In the Wings

– DENISE STEPHANI –

An environmentally friendly book printed and bound in England by
www.printondemand-worldwide.com

This book is made entirely of chain-of-custody materials

www.fast-print.net/store.php

In the Wings
Copyright © Denise Stephani 2012

All rights reserved

No part of this book may be reproduced in any form by photocopying or any electronic or mechanical means, including information storage or retrieval systems, without permission in writing from both the copyright owner and the publisher of the book.

All creative writing characters are fictional. Any similarity to any actual person is purely coincidental

ISBN 978-178035-360-9

First published 2012 by
FASTPRINT PUBLISHING
Peterborough, England.
Printed by Printondemand-Worldwide

The Venus Rising Series

The Trials and Transformation of a Dumb 'Black' Alien Bush Ballerina

Book 1

In The Wings

Trials and Transformation of the Alien Ballerina

Book 2

Behind the Scenes

World Adventures of the Alien Ballerina

Book 3

Butterfly Haven Castle

Alien Bush Ballerina Creates a New World

Also available soon:

Butterfly Journey - Guide to Surviving Abuse and Life Trauma

'The World According to JR' (Jasmine Rose's Life Guide for Women)

'Man Quest for the Modern Knight' (Jasmine Rose's Life Guide for Men)

Children's Books:

Letters to Mandela

The Tale of Butterfly Haven Castle

Ga-nat & Ga-noo & their lost little Ishoo

Denise Stephani

In the Wings

Denise Stephani has been Recognized by Cambridge and Worldwide Who's Who for Excellence in Entertainment Services and honoured as VIP of the Year for 2012

Denise Stephani inspires others through Dance and the Arts

Denise Stephani, Director of the BYCIA Dance and Mixed Media Company, has been recognized by Cambridge & Worldwide Who's Who for showing dedication, leadership and excellence in entertainment services.

Music and dance have made a huge impact on Ms. Stephani's life both professionally and personally. Throughout her 40-year career, first as amateur then professional, she has worked as a performer, dance director, choreographer, producer, entertainment consultant, community artist and educator. She is a survivor of the Apartheid Regime in South Africa; dance was a means of escape from the abuse. She also credits dance for helping her to develop valuable life skills. She created *Butterfly Haven Castle* – a centre for Youth and Survivors and was the Mentor and initiator of the first Chapters of the International Network Free the Children in South Africa. For the past five years Ms. Stephani has worked as the director of the BYCIA Dance and Mixed Media Company. She creates educational programmes to teach others to use dance and the arts as tools for citizenship and to overcome personal issues. On a daily basis, she is responsible for planning social improvement projects and conducting educational workshops.

Ms. Stephani's contributions to the dance field have earned her various awards and honours, including the Royal Academy of Dancing Solo Seal Award, International Vision of Top Talent Award, FNB Vita Award and Most

Denise Stephani

Outstanding Dancer recognition. She is affiliated with Foundation of Community Dance, National Dance Teachers Association and Federation for Small Businesses. As someone who believes in the power of knowledge, she has studied psychology and screenwriting at the University of Edinburgh as well as Therapy, Philosophy, Quantum Metaphysics, Personal Development, Counselling and Transformation Facilitation, Spirituality and Healing through other centres.

For more information about Denise Stephani, visit http://www.denisestephani.com

In the Wings

Denise Stephani BYCIA Dance Company | *Providing mixed media arts prodcuts involving dance, film, writing and theatre for the purposes of Education and Social Improvement services throughout Scotland and internationally.*

Co limited by guarantee – SC401681

(This company is tax registered and is able to recieve funding and donations. Its activities involve Arts and Social Enterprise projects. It is currently hosting Butterfly Haven Children's Fund, which is to be registered as a separate charity if there is sufficient support. More information on page 273)

www.denisestephani.com

Denise Stephani and BYCIA Dance and Mixed Media on:

Youtube, Vimeo, Facebook, Twitter and Tumblr

Denise Stephani

The Venus Rising Series
The Trials and Transformation of an Alien Dumb 'Black' Bush Ballerina

Book 1

In The Wings
Trials and Transformation of an Alien Ballerina

By Denise Stephani

Names, places and times have been changed or omitted to protect privacy

Regarding Creative Writing Sections:
All creative writing characters are fictional. Any similarity to any actual person is purely coincidental

Denise Stephani

Dedicated to The World.

That means

YOU,

Dear Friend.

Thank you for purchasing this book and contributing to the Butterfly Haven Children's Fund.

Thank you for bravely hearing my story within a World Story.

Thank you for being ready to Dance with the truth and all that is happening on Planet Earth right now…within Society, Economy and Environment. The issue which threatens our very existence:

The Culture of Abuse & The Rule of the Bullies…

Thank you for taking the time to learn how the Spirit of Dance and the Arts can help heal many ills, and aid the Evolution of the Community of Humankind

'E<u>ar</u>th' without the '<u>art</u>' is just 'eh'!

(Graffiti quote)

In the Wings

I am but a microcosm of the macrocosm. This is a memoir of one, but the story of many.

I have had a long journey exploring many paths and wisdoms from around the world,

trying to find the sense in life.

Growing up with Abuse in the Apartheid Regime where Christianity dominated, the Bible was the most obvious place to look first:

This is the bible verse that gave me strength on my darkest days and nights of my youth:

> **For God so loved the world that he gave his only begotten son, that whomsoever believes in him shall have eternal light.** John, 3:16

I would read it morning and night, before performances and exams. As a daughter of God, I needed the hope of light and love to guide the way... Something to believe in...

*I wanted to believe that **some kind of intervention** and light was possible.*

I looked to the words of world leaders:

> **'The future depends on what we do in the present.'** - Mahatma Gandhi

I looked in books and films that would express how I was feeling about life and the world:

(From *Breakfast at Tiffany's* by Truman Capote)

Holly Golightly: "How can you bear it? It's a chamber of horrors."

Writer: "Oh you get used to anything," I said annoyed with myself, for actually I was proud of the place.

Holly: **"I don't. I'll never get used to anything. Anybody that does, they might as well be dead".**

And read the words of great poets and philosophers:

Your children are not your children, they are the sons and the daughters of life's longing for itself. They come through you and not from you. They belong not to you. - Khalil Gibran

And I searched the Internet:

Not everything that is faced can be changed, but nothing can be changed until it is faced. - Lucille Ball from *Women Who Change the World*

Overture

Albert Einstein

'Nothing that I can do will change the structure of the universe. But maybe, by raising my voice I can help the greatest of all causes - goodwill among men and peace on earth.'

Maya Angelou

'There is no greater agony than bearing an untold story inside you.'

The Journey of the Butterfly

The butterfly is a glorious creature to look up to when you feel like you need a ladder to get to a worm's level…

What is the path that it travels to become that perfect piece of creation?

Laid from the butt of mother butterfly into a little pile – very cramped inside the tight shell at the bottom of the heap. But the sun shines and the tiny wormlet grows enough to crack the shell of the egg to get out. The other wormlets and eggs are on top of her, but she climbs up between them. The boy wormlets mutter amongst themselves, "Who does she think she is? Sneaky female working her way up and out of her lowly station at the bottom of the heap!" Even most of the other female worms echo, "Sneaky, sneaky, sneaky," like unthinking zombies.

But she smiles sweetly, offers them choice bits of leaf that she brought up with her, and keeps going. She stretches her legs when she has more space and is able to walk free along a branch. She explores her world. But around her she sees the other worms being plucked up by birds – swallowed whole. She hides under a leaf in a branch hollow and watches the competitive fight for survival. Some worms push other worms into the light where the birds can see them so that they will be eaten first. In the fight and tussle for survival some worms fall to their death. A big ugly beetle who is also scared of being eaten decides to keep our little she-worm prisoner in the branch hollow, so that he can grab her and give her to the birds to eat instead of himself. While he keeps her there he taunts her, pokes her and feeds her only enough to keep her alive. Her whole world is dark and brown.

The other worms see what is happening but they ignore her cries for help and pretend that it is not happening. Eventually, after a long time, the beetle gets tired of being in one spot, so he moves away to find another victim to take power over. But just as wormlet is escaping, another ugly beetle comes along and forces and pushes her down the tree trunk and into a tin hidden under one of the big gnarled roots. In the tin are other wormlets, kept prisoner. Boy wormlets too. Our little she-wormlet hears their stories and is very angry. "There are more of us," she says. "We must gang together and rush out screaming! We want colour and joy – not this dark brown world." So this is what they do and the plan works. The beetle is so astonished that he flies away in fear.

Little wormlet is ecstatically happy to escape. She slowly wends her way up the tree and finds juicy leaves and eats her fill – offering to the other worms too. The other worms say suspiciously, "What is wrong with her? Why is she so smiley and giving? Why is she nice and kind? Why does she help others? What does she want?"

In the Wings

She answers as if she is Somebody, not Nobody, as they would have her believe:

"I am not mad or bad. I am just happy to be alive and free!"

"Well we don't like your positive attitude," they say. "It is very strange. Who do you think you are?" They twist her actions into something negative. They scratch and sniff around in the muck and find reasons to ignore her and be against her.

She wonders:

Have I not suffered enough? Can I not just be happy now? Where is compassion? Why are they judging me? They say that the beetle kept me prisoner because I chose it - that maybe I deserved it. That it's my life lesson and burden to bear alone. They didn't help when I called. They chose to be deaf, dumb and blind. They played a part in creating it too. If they had chosen differently it may not have happened, or could have ended long before it did. Now they are all full of talk, but did any of them have the courage to confront the beetle and tell HIM what he was doing was wrong?

She realized that this was because it was far easier to blame the wormlet and take their anger out on her. She had compassion for their fear, even though each time she began to mention her difficult time as a prisoner, they smacked her in the mouth and put a big leaf on top of her to hide her.

What kept wormlet going is that she knew that what was happening to her had happened to many, many others. There were millions and millions – even billions - of little wormlets out there who needed an Ambassador to speak up for them, and help them stand up against the beetles, so that they could no longer get away with their power games. For the Ugly Beetle Games to work there had to be Silence. Sometimes the beetles secretly forced the wormlets to leap off the branches to their death to maintain that permanent Silence. It was a perfect crime.

She needed to end the Great Silence and Sing Out for the greater good of all the suffering wormlets in the world, inspiring them to raise their voices and Sing Out too. She could see that they were all getting sick and dying from the stress of carrying the painful secrets. The toxic, poisonous, brown sorrow festered deep inside them. They needed colour and light.

She felt that she needed to change and become more able in the world and on her mission. She found a quiet branch and started transforming her outer layer into a sturdy safe cocoon. She snuggled in and made herself small and worked on herself. Thinking and meditating and praying.

She connected to the great Divine One and found her path. She dreamed of Heavenly Castle Kingdoms where only Goodness flourished. She was given a golden scroll in a magical chamber which spoke her vision and purpose as a healer. As she changed, her form expanded. Her wings started growing and she felt uncomfortable and cramped in the small space. The safe space was not enough. She needed to move her mission out into the world.

One day she took a deep breath and expanded herself -

cracking open the cocoon.

She eased herself out into the world,

spread her bright rainbow-coloured wings,

In the Wings

fluttered them a little,
and FLEW,
dancing in the sky,
spiralling above the glorious view,
Singing Out wherever she went.

Inspiring others to Sing and Dance too…

Denise Stephani

Prelude

'What would happen if one woman told the truth about her life? The World would split open.'

(Muriel Rukeyser from 'Kathe Kollwitz' and *The Courage to Heal*)

STARTING AGAIN IN SCOTLAND – TRAVELS

February 2007 – Linlithgow, Scotland

I am gazing across the glorious rippling loch towards the majestically rising Linlithgow Palace. The beauty moves me. I see the proud white swans gliding across the water and the music of *The Dying Swan* fills my mind. I want to dance, swirl and fly. I am free at last. I have migrated at long last to the far side of the planet and escaped the shackles of my African existence.

I am in love with the tidy, cared for, safe nature.

I palm the kids off on Hubby and Aunt and go for a rambling explore. It is February and freezing, especially for my thin African blood and ill-equipped wardrobe, but I am breathing in the green plant life, loving the sheep and revelling in the fact that I, as a woman, can actually walk about in nature without worrying about being attacked. Amazing!

This is like a storybook fairytale ending…

Woah - Steady on! What the heck is that?

A quaint olde building with the words 'Black Bitch' emblazoned across it. WTF?

See? I may be staggering through mom-hood, but I'm up with the latest lingo!

(Not sure why it is better than swearing though. Everyone knows what you're saying anyway and it ain't, "What the Fandango?")

Fresh out of South Africa, which nowadays takes PC-ness to the furthest back-bending extremes, and I am confronted by a building that says 'Black Bitch' on it. Meeting house of the Scottish Ku Klux Clan?

Well as it turns out - Hubby's Aunt informed me - they are referring to a female dog with a dark coat. And a legend about misguided loyalty, where the black bitch tried to save its owner, who was a criminal tied up and left to die on the Loch Island.

Mmm... Maybe things are not as calm and lovely as they seem? Never mind, I'm used to that.

Chapter 1

What Happens in the Wings?

'All the world's a stage, and all the men and women merely players' written by the Bard who needs no introduction.

In that case - I want to sack the casting director.

Who chooses which little children are going to be beaten and abused? Probably more than half the world's child population are cast into this role – and for the girl child it is practically automatic.*[1] But all those child players are kept in the wings, even when they grow up, and given very little voice on the world stage. They are permanently locked away in silence... in the land of 'I don't want to know!'

If I were to tell you the full story of my life you would be crying by the time I got to age ten, laughing at the craziness of it all by age twenty, simply not believing me by the time I got to age thirty. You would think I must be deluded and living in a made-up world. Sadly – what I write is all true. When you are thrust into a life full of madness and lies you fully value the truth. 'Truth is stranger than fiction' is one of the truest sayings around.

It's been a life that feels like at least four by now. Like most survivors I feel like I am age four going on four hundred. But don't panic and thrust this book away from you with the usual, 'I don't relate' phrase. I will put in loads of outrageous theatre anecdotes to make the reading

---

[1] Statistics on page 264

easier… God forbid that I should write a 'Misery Tome' - because I know…

'Laugh and the world laughs with you, get abused and you're on your own.'

Cape Town Theatre, 1974

My first ballet! I was elated. I had already been training since just before my fourth birthday and dancing since I could stand. Finally, the day had come that I would see the real thing! At last… six-year-old me watching *Swan Lake*.

As it progressed though, the strongest emotion was not elation, but irritation. I was squirming in my seat. This was not enough for me… to sit here and watch. I wanted to be up there. Doing it!

I was fascinated with the great sweeping curtains that swished to reveal changing scenes, the lighting which set the mood, and the music which filled my tingling ears.

But what interested me more were the skinny curtains lined up at the side and the archways through which the dancers appeared and disappeared. What happened back there… in the wings?

My father was a technician in the theatre so I had already heard stories of the bleeding toes, vomiting and hyperventilating from nerves and exhaustion, the oxygen tanks and the hard hours of work. Also the strange arty, decadent people, and their scandalous affairs, parties and drugs - my father didn't believe in censoring this sort of thing for me. In fact he relished and embellished the stories as he made us listen in his smoke-filled bedroom…

as he sucked and twirled the end of a sweaty, saliva-spotted marijuana joint.

I didn't find the decadence appealing at all - in fact I found it rather sickening - but I had already learned by then to take what he said with a shovelful of salt... this was my dream and I was going to fulfil it. To one day be up there twirling, jumping, sliding... poised to create a beautiful line... and twirl again. So what if it was hard and painful and the beautiful images of perfection were an illusion! Life was hard and painful and illusory - I had learnt this already - but at least at the Ballet there was magic and beauty, sometimes...

And anyway - this was something I had decided I wanted to do before I met my father, and I had promised myself by now that I wasn't going to let his behaviour affect me!

He was a fairly recent development in my life. My father saw me once as a baby, deserted us, and then turned up on our doorstep again after years of silence and no support when I was nearly five. My mother finally got her *Mills & Boon* happy ending and secretly married my father... a dangerous stranger.

They had originally met at a 'Session' disco in Pretoria in the sixties. Mary had gone with some of her nursing colleagues on a night off. She was beautiful and stylish, all five-feet-and-practically-nothing of her, and could be painfully shy. A little dark-haired, pint-sized morsel bopping gingerly to the sixties beat. She looked across the room avoiding eye contact with her dance partner and instead, to her horror, made contact with a sexily gyrating, long-haired feral youth. Tom was on the scene.

(She often described how she had such an overwhelming sense of destiny. She said she actually dreamt about him before she met him. She had a dream vision about standing with him under a blossoming cherry tree.)

When she saw him in real life she froze, and first felt fear. Then a thought came to her that he couldn't make her do anything she didn't want. She started laughing and laughing until her bewildered dance partner disappeared and suddenly she found herself dancing with Tom.

(This was an ironic beginning to the ongoing pattern - since somehow he had already made her dance with him without even asking, and she continued to dance to his tune.)

Mary was an upper middle-class, church-going Afrikaner from a good area of Johannesburg who also spoke fluent English, German and a smattering of Dutch. The family came from the cultured wine farming people of Franschoek in the Cape, originally émigrés who had escaped religious persecution in Holland.

Her father was a top engineer and quiet genius.

Tom was from a lower middle-class Afrikaner family who came from a less classy area of Pretoria. His family was originally from Luxembourg and Denmark but apparently there was some connection, way back, to Danish nobility.

She was the dutiful, ladylike daughter.

He had run away from home permanently at the age of fifteen, after previous escapes, and was now basically a hippy child of the sixties. (Although that was just a useful disguise. There was nothing truly peace-loving or hippy about him!)

This was a large part of the appeal for Mary: the 'Princess and the Pauper' image...

Have you noticed how people put EVERYTHING into tables nowadays? It's a disease of the computer revolution – so I thought I would 'do as in Rome' and give you a Differences Table for clarity.

Table listing Tom and Mary differences:

Tom	Wild	Lower Middle-Class	Promiscuous	Psychopathic South African Lightweight Champion Boxer/ Electrical Technician trainee
Mary	Mild	Upper Middle-Class	Conservative	Zero self-esteem, but very intelligent, conservative Trainee Nurse / Artist

They dated for approximately a year before I was conceived. He had apparently been a gentleman (i.e. biding his time) up to this point, respecting my mother's conservative Christian attitude to sex. But one day he created a situation where they were alone in his parents' house and raped her. That is her side of story but he just shrugged and laughed when I confronted him with it. Isn't it amazing how evil and dismissive laughter can be?

So I am an unwanted product of rape.

My grandparents were horror-struck when they came back from a holiday trip overseas and saw that their perfect little daughter had a bump fast developing. They totally disapproved of my father, and hinted darkly at some scandalous history that his family was involved in. (I never found out what, but a 'touch of the tar brush' or incest I suspect.) They obviously felt really strongly about it because despite their conservative 'churchiness' they refused to let them marry. They insisted that the best plan would be for me to be adopted, and for Mary and Tom not to see each other.

This was all happening in racist Apartheid South Africa: Strange happenings in a strange place in a strange time.

Jasmine Rose:

Now is maybe a good time to introduce my very great friend Jasmine Rose. She has been with me over the years - through all the ups and downs, held my hand and comforted me in my darkest hours. What makes her so special is that she has a completely outrageous way of looking at the world and is not scared to voice it in spunky terms. She is full of strange facts, perspectives and insights, which can feel a bit like a grenade being thrown at you – but can also really make you laugh. Thank goodness for Jasmine.

But first I have to give you a pre-reading disclaimer notice as they do at the beginning of films with contentious content:

Jasmine's opinions are:

'for entertainment purposes only and don't necessarily reflect the opinions' of the author. Perhaps to be taken with a pinch of salt…

Here are some of her classic insights which entertained me in a dark hour:

Denny, I have been having some Thoughts on Creation. Listen to this new interesting fact:

We all know that the elephant has the hugest dong imaginable and it actually drags along the ground behind it when extended. However – apparently, it is not used for penetration since the female elephant has a very short and small vagina. So instead, about a litre of sperm just gets sprayed in the general direction of the opening.

What kind of a cosmic joke is that? Whoever created all this was really trying to raise laughs! The biggest dong on land (whales get the general size award) and it just has a spray-hose function rather than a jackhammer, drive-it-home function. The females get to look at this long dong but don't get any action from it…

I actually don't know which concept is more ridiculous. The sticking it in? Or the not sticking it in, and just spraying it about? It all just seems so silly.

Urgh! I hope I don't die and then find out that I played a huge role in the master plan and design on the other side, before I chose to be born here and experience it all… it would just be too embarrassing. So much on this planet seems like a nice idea on paper but absolutely sucky and plain horrible in reality!

The programme this elephant info came from also went on to show that elephants have pregnancies of twenty-two months, but dogs in that time can produce three litters of up to ten pups...

Ow! – either way. Pregnancy is not a blessed state. A torturously long one, or rapid short ones with huge numbers, both sound like horrible cruel torture to me. Anyone who has been pregnant and hasn't got Mom-nesia straight afterwards would know exactly what I mean.

Us females really 'get' the imperfectness of this creation, yet we get lumbered with male partners who demand that we admire their perfection at all times no matter what trouble they bring us. Bizarre!

The only way that any of this (and all that is going on in the world right now) can make sense, is if we are in the middle of an On-going Creation and are still Co-creating to get to a better end point. Shame that we're messing it up so badly.

See what I mean? What a treasure! Wrestling with outrageous and intriguing universal conundrums like that can take one's mind off one's misery quite effectively.

So there were adoptive parents 'waiting in the wings' at my birth.

But when I popped out my mother did an about-turn and insisted on keeping me. She was obviously very in love with my father and knew that giving away his child would be a finite act of rejection of him too.

She regularly manipulated me with it though, and made me feel like I should be grateful to be alive at all. She told me horrific stories when I was very little about how women stick knitting needles up themselves to abort their children. She told me that I was lucky not to have met a similar fate – so 'co-operate or else'. I had to be 'the good, compliant little girl at all costs' and that set up a situation of very effective manipulation for years to come.

So many millions of children out there in the world are made to feel that they are being tolerated on sufferance. Why is that?

Jasmine would say: *If you don't really want to be bothered with children, don't stick it in!*

Jasmine Rose has always been very comforting about my inauspicious entry. She says things like:

I wouldn't be at all surprised if a birth story like yours is similar to the true story of Jesus which has been turned into the exaggerated Immaculate Conception story. Poor Mary probably got raped while collecting water at the well and Joseph was decent enough to stand by her, marry her and be a good husband and father anyway. Then greatness shone through with the child Jesus even after a stable birth. That is a miraculous enough story in itself!

It was probably originally a Moral Tale with the point being that special people can come to Earth through the least auspicious route, and should be valued equally to anyone else.

C'mon people – play along! We've all played Broken Telephone or seen how stories get distorted and embellished. This is Planet Earth and the human race we're talking about after all!

It's all about selective storytelling and embellishment for dubious purposes. What's that saying? 'Never spoil a good story with the truth.'

My Moral Tale Theory works too. The message being that community needs to take responsibility for all children no matter how they arrive on planet Earth – and you never know what they might become! It takes a village to protect a child and let it flower to its highest potential...

I was born prematurely in a hospital laundry closet because the birth was so quick that they couldn't get my mother into the delivery room in time. I must have been very keen to be born and welcomed into the experience of this world.

Mary realized that my father probably had a lot of growing up to do still, so she suggested he did his own thing for a while, and wait and see if they still wanted to marry later. He went off in a huff and disappeared for nearly five years. My grandparents tried to trace him through the police to get maintenance but he was well hidden in the drug haze of the hippy communes of Cape Town.

So I grew up with my grandparents and my mother. Nobody gave me a proper explanation about my father so I resorted to making things up when the other children at Nursery School asked me where my father was... 'He got sick and died', 'He was on an adventure', 'He was coming back to marry my mother with a big wedding in a beautiful church with flowers'...

I longed for a father.

Then one day just before my fifth birthday he did arrive at the room that my mother and I shared in a house near her work. He arrived with a blue stuffed toy dog. This was supposed to make me like him. I did make a real attempt for my mother's sake but the dog became 'Poo-fy'. I made a game of making the dog 'poo' on Tom. That was the truest expression for what I was feeling. I sensed trouble. The 'kak' was about to hit the fan... but as a four-year-old I didn't have the words to express it, the power to be heard, or any choice in the matter. (Oops – little swear word kak slipped in there. But it is 'poo' in Afrikaans so I think I can get away with it?)

Jasmine would interject in this part of the story and say:

What a pile of dog-doo. Don't you just want to punch those prosy self-helpers who say: 'There is always choice'?

My mother told me that he had asked her to marry him and that in a few days' time we would go to Pretoria to the civil courts for the wedding. She spent the night before crying and fretting.

I wish that she had at least slowed down to think. I wish she had realized that butterflies in the tummy can mean fear, not love, and the two are easily confused... but I guess it seemed like the perfect romantic happy ending.

So in her mind we were united as a little family. Mary and Tom - Princess and the Underdog - united against the world. But they were dragging me unwillingly in their wake and now I had a horrible feeling in my tummy all the time...

My wonderful godfather, Mickey, had been madly in love with my mother for years and was a favourite uncle/father substitute to me. He and his mother owned and ran the

In the Wings

Nursery School that I had gone to from about six months of age. He was so shocked by the unexpected turn of events that he fled Johannesburg and went to Rhodesia (now Zimbabwe) where he had a farm. His sudden disappearance was absolutely devastating to me. Things were already getting rather scary for me at home and now my Uncle Mickey was gone too.

I remember one day at the Nursery school:

I was in a total state - crying and crying. My pants elastic had snapped, my pants kept falling down and I just wanted him to fix things, hold me and make everything okay - but he was gone. The emotional agony was unbearable. I walked around wailing like a lost soul, trying to keep everything in place - weeping and weeping, "I want Uncle Mickey!" I think I remember it so well because it was the last time I was allowed to cry like that no matter what happened to me.

I don't know what had made my pants' elastic snap - maybe just rough handling which I was already getting a lot of. I was being trained to know the difference between a 'Right Jab', 'Hook Left' and 'Disorientating Smack against the Head'. Tom had a hero in Mohammed Ali so he liked to 'Float like a butterfly and STING LIKE A BEE'.

But I do also have a very clear memory of the first stirrings of sexual abuse that happened at that time. Due to some minor offence (like putting my shoes on the wrong way around) I was being given a hiding in the bathroom. He was sitting on the edge of the bath and I was hauled across his lap, face down, and he had pulled my pants down. He was creating a whole ceremony out of this event - high as a kite no doubt.

He ran water into the basin and took his time rubbing and smearing some across my buttocks, massaging it into the cheeks, and telling me that it was to make it sting more when he hit me with a brush. I felt examined and sniffed at - it was like a cat playing with the mouse and examining the spoils before it seriously attacks. My innocent five-year-old little mind went, Oho, there is something sick and perverted happening here!

Now let me just say at this point that children don't 'imagine' this kind of thing for nothing. In those days nobody talked about child abuse and I most certainly didn't know anything about sex. It was before TV in South Africa. But to the depth of my soul I knew that there was something very wrong happening here and that he wanted something.

Can you believe that there are people who try to say that perhaps incest and child sexual abuse is okay and that it is just some cultures and conditioning that makes it not okay? (Even church and community leaders!) All I can tell you is that nobody had conditioned me into anything of that nature by that age. It hadn't even been a question - but in that first more subtle invasion, my soul was screaming. It was not fun, it was not nice and it was a totally unwanted invasion. Most children would say the same.

Stop for a minute and imagine being sexually molested or raped by a 20-foot giant.

I've been told that children make 'a big thing' of it. You would not believe what people have said to me over the years. It IS a big thing! Comparatively speaking his thing would be huge – as big as your leg. The rest of him would be massive and heavy and probably smell really bad… and it would hurt, body, mind and soul. Little children are torn to pieces – left to die, or suffer for life with patched-up, irreparably damaged internal organs.

Imagine being beaten by someone four or five times your size. Think what it would be like to have something the size of your own leg shoved up you!

It's amazing how people come up with all kinds of kakky, fucked-up reasons why it is okay so that they don't have to think about it or get involved. It's not okay – it's never okay.

Okay – you've picked up that I swear a little bit. My inner dialogue is full of swearing thanks to a father that used the 'f' and 's' words as nouns, verbs, adjectives and just for general sprinkling.

But even a Duchess should swear at the amount of abuse to the extreme that is going on, on this planet at the moment. We are seeing Abuse Attitudes in families, communities, economy and environment!

Right – I've had a little rant – time for a theatre anecdote to lighten the mood…

My first role as a professional ballet dancer was very glamorous. (Not!)

I was the last chicken in the row in La Fille Mal Gardée. *La Fille is a gorgeous, frothy, quirky, romantic comedy with lots of lovely, graceful choreography.*

My poultry role was not graceful at all. I was encased in a huge chicken body and head, with limited vision through some mesh under the beak, and my skinny legs in stripy yellow tights sticking out underneath. One of the male dancers was a cocky rooster who herded us four little new ballerina chicks in a comical dance. Even though the audience enjoyed it and I laugh now, we were terrified and embarrassed by it all.

It didn't quite fit in with our ballerina dreams! We had a tough time with our vision challenge to know where we were going, and to stay out of the way of the REAL horse and carriage in the ballet. We toured to Windhoek, capital city of Namibia, and there the horse was plain insane.

It made its entrance onto the stage just after us, and as the 'last-chicken-in-the-row' I had a tough time hanging onto my tail feathers. The horse kept biting my tail so I had to stand to one side in the wings, and then make an ultra-quick leaping jeté *forward, past the horse, to get onto stage - with its yellow teeth flashing behind me.*

One performance it got irritated with my successful tail protection tactics, so it dropped a present in my path a little later on in the scene, and I chicken-danced mad-horse manure all over the stage!

A more embarrassing thing happened on that tour to one of the soloists which cheered us little hens up no end. She got arrested for shop-lifting. She and another ballerina were gossiping so hard in the main supermarket of Windhoek that she forgot that she had looked at a T-shirt, then draped it over her arm ― so she walked out without paying. She was brutally arrested by the store detective and locked in the toilets until the police came!

It was quite a scandal for the company because there had been big banners across the main street saying, 'Welcome PRETORIA Ballet', a Gala event with the mayor and all the dignitaries, press interviews, TV etc. And now one of us was exposed as a scabby criminal. Bad Ballerinas Abroad!

She was not allowed to leave the country with the rest of us, and had to sign a confession and pay a fine, so that she could get back to SA in time to dance a leading role. That's dancer dedication for you. She would rather get a false criminal record than miss her chance at a main role and let her many fans down!

Yup. That's right. There is a 'rags-to-riches' tale here - or 'sucky-ness to success' anyway - but it would take at least another fifteen years to unfold, so I will take you back to my five-year-old youth…

Everything was horrible. I was dragged along to gangster-ish boxing halls and to score *dagga* (marijuana) in creepy places.

I was pulled along at high speed with a weird handhold Tom insisted on – linked little fingers. My little digit felt like it was being wrenched off, my toes bleeding because of stubbing them while being dragged along at that pace. He screamed at me, telling me it was my fault and to 'lift my feet' or he'd beat me for bleeding.

He was forever digging his fingers into my neck or upper arm or squashing my little hand in his calloused boxer's hands till I thought the bones would crack. But he would tell me that if I showed that I was in pain or cried he would take me home and give me a hiding. So I learnt to ignore pain, wear a mask, and act at a very early age. To him it was nothing - just a way to get what he wanted and to feel powerful.

All the secrets also began then. Trips to the drug dealer and the return journey with the drugs stuffed into my pants. I was a drug mule. He even stopped and chatted to some policemen once and I was terrified that I would be arrested and locked up.

Then later he would brag about it to his druggie friends and get me to show how I roll a joint for him… A party trick from the 'performing monkey' to boost his fractured ego: I soon learnt that to survive I had to be useful and 'perform' for his purposes.

Chapter 2

Cycling the Cycle

Ouma's Afrikaans saying: *Die voeltjies van die hemel het hulle gatte op ons gedraai*

Translation: The angels of heaven have turned their arses on us.

STARTING AGAIN IN SCOTLAND - TRAVELS

2009 South Queensferry and Incholm Abbey

I take the boys, go for a trip over to Incholm Abbey:

We set off on the ferry from South Queensferry and sail across the Forth to Incholm Island. Dotted like jewels on the shoreline are *Staghead Hotel*, Orocco Pier and *Hawe's Inn* where I sometimes stay and write - following in the footsteps of Robert Louis Stevenson.

It's a lovely day (for Scotland).

There is something so relaxing about floating on the gentle waters of a wide river or loch. Water has always given me comfort.

The abbey glows in the sunlight and the island is a child's paradise. We feel like we are in a *Famous Five* story. There are Second World War bunkers and a tunnel through the hill to explore. We imagine that we are secret agents hanging out. Great fun!

The abbey is a maze of spaces and rooms and the only way up the tower is a narrow, snug, dwarf-size spiral staircase - only for little people.

("Definitely wouldn't feature in the Fat Olympics," joke the un-PC boys.)

We spiral up the steep staircase, reaching the top to admire the view and the drop.

Something called me here... I have been drawn to this place.

I am touched by the thought of living a peaceful life here. Simple living. Writing, study, prayer. Being spiritual. What a blessing it would be...

The only problem, we agree, is that on planet Earth it would be bound to all fall apart and be riddled with politics and nonsense of The Horrible Humans.

That is how Incholm Abbey ended... it was destroyed by wars.

Not fun at all...

I am inviting you to do some quantum time-travelling with me. I am taking you leaping forward and back in time in this story. In my life, linear time became scrambled. I was living in my happier past, and projecting decades ahead into the future to survive. In my bed at night I visualized myself in other places on my personal time-line. I am taking you further back in time to understand the back story which I understood from very young...

Tom's Story:

Now is perhaps the time to tell you some of his story. How he became this fractured ego on legs. He was also a victim... and a victim of victims. If I merely continue with all the horror stories you will see him as a monster with yellow, blood-dripping fangs and not as the damaged human like you and me. What he did is monstrous and he was a raging psychopath, but he was a sweet little baby boy once, who was turned into a monster by his family and life. He had some good sides and great intentions. Unfortunately he was stuck in a pattern of rage and bad choices and imposed them on others.

All I can tell you is the bits that I remember being told over the years. I don't know how much is true or exaggerated since Tom tends never to 'spoil a good story with the truth', but there were certain stories that were told repeatedly and they stuck. We were very cut off from all family and I saw them only occasionally, but from what I saw of them the stories made sense. My mother was forever justifying his behaviour, and telling me that I must understand that he had a difficult childhood, that he didn't know any better. Here is the story. See what you think...

Tom was born into a paranoid post-war society. Yes - South Africa was affected too. The whole world is affected by the antics of the First World and its wars. Throw a stone into a pond and there is a ripple effect, especially in the Colonies of European Imperialism.

Tom used to say that the community that he grew up with were *verkramp* – in a permanent cramp - conservative, dour, mean-spirited, fearful and nasty. There was a tendency toward harsh religious zeal balanced by underground deviance.

My grandmother's pregnancy must have been terrible. For some reason my grandfather rejected my father and said that Tom wasn't his child. It only became clear to me much later what the problem was: Tom's dark-toned skin, genes from the throwback French/Spanish blood, within a racist, anti-black society.

Tom's father was very jealous and possessive of my grandmother, Rita. She was glamorous and attractive and she sang in their band. He didn't like the thought of sharing her - even with fans or a child. He was a horrible, cruel, mean-spirited old man and he gave me the creeps. He was rude and violent towards his wife and child. I found him revolting and my mother and I dreaded his slobbery, brandy kisses and gropes.

The birth of Tom was a drawn-out, three-day ordeal - probably because Rita was in fear - and Tom felt so unwelcome. He was born on Friday the thirteenth (a fact he wasn't allowed to forget. He felt cursed from the moment he was born.)

He spent a great deal time with his *Ouma* (grandmother) because he wasn't welcome at home. When he was five he was sent to wrestling and boxing classes. It was time for him to prove that he was worthy of his father's attention by becoming a fighting machine! He was forced to boost the fragile ego of his father. As he grew a little older it became clear that boxing was more his forte. He was soon winning cups and championships. Getting himself beaten up to prove that he was worth something to his father. That's what *okes* (blokes) and *manne* (men) did.

Self-worth through violence. And so the patterns repeat...

He spent a lot of time just trying to get out of the house. They lived near a mountain ridge and he would disappear into the mountains all day and would even sleep there at night, despite the fact that there were occasional leopards and wild cats on the prowl. He knew the different edible wild fruits growing on the mountain. He learnt how to catch a guinea fowl, wrap it in clay and bake it on a fire. A survivor from a long line of pioneering survivors.

There is a book written by a respected professor about an ancestor of mine who survived the Battle of Blood River, losing his entire family when he was a boy, then getting lost in the wilderness, and surviving through his talents with bees and hunting. He later met up with a weaker tribe escaping the Zulus and helped them get away with intelligent tactics. He stayed with the tribe and contributed with the gifts which came with being an animal and nature lover, but eventually made it back to civilization. So it is strong stock connected to the wild that Tom came from.

There was an odd angle to Tom's relationship with his mother because he told stories of how he used to go to the local boutique and buy clothes for his mother. Maybe it was because she was a virtual prisoner in the home? She was in her husband's obsessive clutches most of the time. She also worked in his hairdressing salon. There was no freedom or respite for her.

She was a hostage locked into that subtle, not-so-subtle enslavement of women in marriage.

To prove himself Tom also became a rugby star at his school. One day in class he punched a teacher so that he flew across the room crashing into the blackboard and slumping unconscious to the floor. This was excused without punishment because he was one of the key players in the team. The principal pretended to give him a caning by hitting a telephone book so that Tom wouldn't be put off his game! They wanted to win the Transvaal Administrator's Cup - and that was more important than deviant behaviour. In fact, deviant behaviour and a few sneaky fouls were just what they needed to win. That was the way of it in Afrikaner Man-World of *manne* and *okes*… (guys)

Was this the beginning of a pattern of Tom getting away with negative behaviour and people covering up for him, even using and applauding his behaviour? He was certainly very proud of the story and told it repeatedly.

Jasmine's comment:

The thing is that he was popular despite being an obvious rebel, womaniser and reprobate. He managed to secure a following and fans. He manipulated life so that he was admired. Even his bad behaviour he sold to be admirable. How did he do it? How did he manage to make it look cool? Or is it simply that society is so sick that they turned a blind eye or even applauded his actions? He had women, homosexuals and African people who were his willing slaves despite the fact that he was proudly sexist, homophobic and racist. Quite bizarre when you think about it…

If there had been appropriate justice with a long-term jail sentence he probably would have had loonies writing to him and a whole fan base of women. Look at all the insane women swooning over Heathcliff in Wuthering Heights. *A totally abusive psychopath but the women have been trained over the eons to find that sexy. It's like collective Stockholm Syndrome.*

Psychopathic behaviour in men is condoned and applauded. Men find it admirable and cool. Women find it sexy. Sick! Instead of being warned about bad men in plays like A Streetcar Named Desire *by Tennessee Williams, women are titillated and the* manne *copy.*

In the Wings

The men in the family were also expected to be part of the racist Apartheid chauvinist male *Broederbond*. (Brotherbond: An organisation which was like a cross between the Ku Klux Klan and the Freemasons. They were a boy's club that kept all power, contacts and business for White Afrikaner males only.)

When Tom was in his early teens he used to stay with his aunt in the house next door whenever her husband was away on business to be company and protection. Apparently very odd things happened next door. The neighbourhood kids used to spy on his aunt having sex with her Alsatian! One day she tried to seduce Tom. He was already acting outside of norms himself and was dating both of his female cousins, but he was shocked and ran. (Not surprisingly, since he had just seen her doing it with a dog!) He told his father who screamed that he was a liar and beat him up. So - at the age of fifteen – he ran away from home. He was already in his final school year, since he had started school early and was very bright with an exceptionally high IQ. Because of this unfair event, he didn't get the opportunity to write the exams, which he resented. He had a chip on his shoulder about it for decades. Was this the start of his War Against Women?

Jasmine Rose:

Eeergh! The cross-critter-sex thing is far more common than one would like to think – a whole other angle to animal cruelty... Well - the whole thing was cruel. No wonder he was so messed up.

He hiked down to Natal and stayed in the mountains there. He lived near a Zulu tribal village and he would swap portrait drawings for food. At some stage he lived in a Hindu temple for six weeks, was vegetarian and did much soul-searching. He told tales of his explorations and had very interesting books. Unfortunately the peaceful philosophies didn't stick.

He was at the top of the lightweight boxing division before he left home and at some point he went back into civilization and started boxing again. He became South African Amateur Lightweight Champion, but he had made himself a promise to give up when he was knocked out because he didn't want to become a brain-damaged cabbage. His last fight was with someone well above his weight. He was paid by gangsters to fight with the knowledge that he would probably lose. He was knocked out and he retired then and there.

He drifted around doing various things, making and selling belts at the hippy flea markets in Hillbrow and doing promotions for the Circus. He trained in electrical engineering and the Police Force. His stories were wild and intriguing. He told us a police story about when his team found a body a couple of weeks old and he and a fellow trainee had tried to lift and move the body. Tom grabbed the ankles enthusiastically ready to heave and lift - but the flesh squirted gorily, like salsa with guacamole, between his fingers, making him heave his lunch instead! I remember being grossed out for years over that one.

Tom was full of anecdotes. He did life at full throttle and he truly wanted to be a hero.

Once, when I was about twelve he was in his boss's car driving down Adderly Street, when he saw a man with a gun holding up a queue of people waiting for a bus. The car was moving but he told the driver to slow down and he jumped out, knocked the guy out with one punch, grabbed the gun, and jumped back in the car. Very filmic. I can just imagine the faces of the people involved and the comments of the witnesses. It must have seemed like some caped avenger had swooped in and left like a comic superhero. Tom's outfit was usually a shirt undone right to the waist showing off his impressive boxer's chest, way-too-tight jeans with thick belt and boots, his shoulder length hair flying in the wind. The witnesses must have thought that it was a real gun, but it turned out that it was a criminal-marking dye gun with purple ink for self-defence, so Tom was marked for weeks after.

He had his entertaining, and even good sides. He helped quite a number of people along the way, but he destroyed far more. The anger, rage and cruelty were consistently simmering beneath the surface. He could switch from angelic to demoniac in the blink of a gargoyle's eye.

I looked at his dye-marked purple hands and wished that the police would arrest him.

Denisestephani@god: Are we all hamsters on the treadmill repeating cycles into eternity? Is it possible to jump off?

Jasmine Rose:

Sigh - The only thing you learn from history is that people don't learn from history, dearie.

Mary's Story:

My mother's story is relatively typical for any girl born in the mid-forties. She was disempowered with all sorts of oppressive brainwashing. You have to be ladylike... take little steps, sit with your legs together and feet to the side. It doesn't matter whether you're top of the class, women can't become doctors or vets. It's a man's world. Marry a professional, preferably from dad's work etc. etc.

Yeeurgh! But apart from this her family life was great compared to mine. Her father was a wonderful, intelligent, decent man, who provided well for his family. To be fair, he was maybe a gentle OCD control freak. High-functioning Asperger's I suspect. Autism with high IQ which is becoming more and more common. Being very short, he had been bullied badly at school. He was my sweet little *Oupa* (grandfather).

Her mother was slightly potty. As a toddler Mary had to go through the excruciating business of having her hair curled daily… which I would call a 'safe' form of physical abuse! But half the female population at the time had to endure it. Her mother was definitely obsessive, and a manic depressive, becoming a full-on housebound, depressive hypochondriac in the second half of her life. She came from a family of ten kids and was a secretary before she married. I always thought that leaving her job and retiring to be an isolated, bored, housewife and raise children was a big part of the problem. It was probably undiagnosed postnatal depression. This is a massive unspoken problem for women. Actress Gwyneth Paltrow has recently very bravely spoken about her battle with it, and how she understands that it never fully goes away.

I think that my *Ouma's* (grandmother's) life felt plain boring and purposeless. For forty years she said she was dying of cancer, despite the fact that she was actually as healthy as a horse. The doctors, who kept telling her that she was okay, were 'a bunch of quacks'. She didn't have any friends. *Ouma* spent her time either playing Mary and her brother up against each other or going into a decline and staying in her room, in her gown, for days on end.

In the Wings

Despite his general wonderfulness *Oupa* must have been very hard to be married to. He was one of those introverted, quiet genius types. He was an engineer for the *SABC* and was involved in important projects such as the placing and design of the radio towers and communication systems involving sound waves.

He tended to take things apart, creating technology, or do woodwork - generally pottering around the place. I think it was hard to connect properly with him on a personal level which was frustrating for the family females. He was all about chores and doing – not much about feeling, despite being sensitive and gentle. But I loved *Oupa* to bits. I recall him showing me a prism and explaining the rainbow effect. He spoke of how light waves and sound waves worked as the two of us tinkered about in his workshop. I also loved to bang away on the big black typewriter in his office.

Ouma and *Oupa* were both very conservative and upstanding and always 'right'. They constantly fretted about 'what the people would think'. It is no wonder Mary wanted to rebel and prove them wrong. The 'right/wrong' and 'what will they think' issues were to have a major negative impact on the rest of her life… and mine.

Mary got straight As at school and was an avid learner. She had inherited the brains. She sat at the front of the class absorbing as much as she could, even taking on extra subjects. She was good at languages and a natural academic who wanted to go to university and study medicine or a veterinary science. Her parents said no. Money was to be spent on sending her younger brother to university, not her. To study to be a doctor or vet would be 'unladylike'.

I can imagine the fury, rage and frustration that she must have felt. She was sent off to nursing college instead. Might as well have been the salt mines. She was consigned to horrendous working hours, low pay and little appreciation. 'No status for a female, thank you very much. Use your brains to pretend that you're stupid and catch a man instead' was essentially the message.

Jasmine Rose:

What she needed to do was grow a dick. Just a few extra inches of flesh between her legs is what she needed. Freud and his penis envy! It's not the penis that we want – although they can be handy - it's the power and the privileges. It has been scientifically proven that we are all female to start with and the male mutation only starts happening a few weeks into the foetal development. Read Why Men Don't Listen And Women Can't Read Maps *by Allan & Barbara Pease. It's brilliant!*

But despite being the blueprint of life and global majority, do you know that to this day women are only allowed to earn approximately 10% of the world's income and own less than 1% of the world's property, despite being the major workforce? Most of that 1% is probably taken up by the Queen, Oprah and various film stars. Everyone is very good at 'the talk' regarding women's rights and equality achieved, but those are the harsh facts from Oxfam. *Equality is in The Land of Far, Far Away.*

In the current World Order, people with no economic power have no say. That is why the mutant dick-features still rule supreme and work like heck to maintain the status quo.

Any visiting intelligent, observing alien would be reeling at the injustice of it all! No wonder they haven't made proper contact yet!

Well, it is no wonder that Mary was ripe for the plucking when a charming psycho found her - anything to give her family the finger. They absolutely hated and disapproved of him. How satisfying for her! That is how women often get into these abuse situations. They are in difficult, vulnerable life circumstances, with no support, and the predators sniff it out and pounce. It's that lone wounded animal straying from the pack that gets pounced on. The pity is that parents don't warn properly because they want to keep girls naïve, and they prefer to say, "I told you so," after.

Yes. My mother was a victim of the Gender War, which made her a weakened target for an Alpha Male parasite to step in and perpetrate Gender Violence on her and her daughter.

---

jasminerose@facebook

What do the Angels, or intelligent aliens think of this planet, looking at it from an objective distance? The Planet of Boys-with-their-toys floating in a space-zone of poor priorities! We have a total imbalance of society in so many ways, and are destroying our own environment as fast as we can - like cancer on the planet. No wonder there is so much cancer, especially breast cancer. It reflects the destruction of the feminine and female values. It is a reflection within the bodies of the microcosm, demonstrating what is happening in the macrocosm. Gender Dis-ease. Any comments peeps?

The Pretoria Theatre: Late Eighties

One evening during a heartrending performance of Giselle, *we had an unexpected moment which left the* corps de ballet *weak at the knees with laughter:*

After the tragic mad scene and death of Giselle the villagers are weeping and wailing as Prince Albrecht exits over the bridge out of the village. The lying, using, two-timing Prince, who is already engaged to a princess is trying to get one in with the commoners before he is stifled by marriage. He flees in disgrace!

Only to pause on the bridge, dramatically, looking back with a tiny inkling of regret...

The only problem was that on this night the techies had forgotten to put the brakes on the bridge wheels, so when he leapt melodramatically onto it, the bridge took off at high speed.

It exited into the wings with the prince stumbling and hanging onto the rustic rails for dear life.

It's fortunate for us corps de ballet *members that laughing can look like weeping from a distance. The corps was corpsing. Management would have killed us if we hadn't been able to pull off a good cover-up!*

Jasmine Rose:

Ah, but what happens in life? The Princes use us and make us weep and drive us potty, break our hearts, and we cover up with a tight smile.

In the Wings

The Princes are hardly ever seen to look back with regret. There is never good and gory justice where a bunch of mean Willis (yes, pronounced willies) spirits of betrayed dead women make him dance to near death and repent for his sins...

Although there are sometimes women vigilante groups who take action...

Well – the brakes were off on Mary's bridge too. She would be careering about hanging on for dear life, fearing death for the rest of her life because the Bridge/Prince she chose to leap onto was a maniac bucking bronco.

Here is another table I made up to explain them to you (and myself):

Tom	Very High IQ	Clever, conniving, hard-working job excellence when it suits/ Lazy as hell when it doesn't	King Complex: Gets everyone to 'do' for him	I understand what went wrong for him. Direct Damage and unwillingness to deal with it.
Mary	High IQ	Intelligent and hard-working, good at her job. Angel of the wards.	Princess complex: transformed into Cinderella in the ashes. A woman who does too much.	I don't fully understand what went wrong for her. Pride, stubbornness and an unwillingness to be wrong were her downfall. A rebellion against oppressive sexist attitudes gone wrong...

So there I was - stuck with my hellish parents…

I am sure you are starting to wonder where spirituality and religion fit in with all of this. Dealing with it all definitely put me on the path of spiritual and existential questioning. I have given life much thought. When you are going through seven types of hell it makes you think and pray – A LOT. 'No atheists in a foxhole' people. I prayed Very High Quality Prayers. Some major intense tweets went out to Twitter God of the *Google* in the sky, I can assure you. I was ready to socially connect with anyone in the universe who could help me out of the darkness and bring some light to my life. But many people have made me feel like it happened to me because I was doing something wrong.

Jasmine Rose goes off on a tangent:

Don't you absolutely hate it when people try to tell you that horrible things happened to you because you didn't pray properly, or your connection to God is somehow inferior, and then they stand praying all over you. Like they have the hotline! They are completely rude and invasive power-trippers. Whenever that happens, I get the same shocked, invaded feeling as I get when I'm at the beach and a randy dog suddenly sniffs up behind me sticking it's snout up my butt, then tries to go for a mount.

Sometimes shit just happens randomly to random people - or because of family and community patterns and dysfunction. It is totally puerile to crap on and power-pray over individual victims who have already been through enough, simply to shut them up or to have an ego-trip!

Imagine doing that to a survivor of the 9/11 terror attack? It would be too rude!

In the Wings

I was personally touched and devastated by 9/11 because I lost a friend who was giving a presentation in one of the rooftop function areas of the Twin Towers. We buried the remains that they found with a non-religious spiritual celebration of his life, under a spreading tree on his family farm in Cape Town. We hugged his parents, ate with them and empathized, offering our own private prayers for his spirit, respectfully, at his graveside.

To me all war, terror and violence is abuse. Abuse of power, lives and resources. And when people say that God is on their side in the killing, rape and pillage - then they abuse the Lovely Creator/Creation.

denisestephani@facebook: likes 'Breaking the Cycle of Abuse' ☺

I was born into a family of Dutch Reformed churchgoers. Except that they didn't go to church any more once they were cursed with my presence. When my grandmother found out that Mary was pregnant with me she loudly proclaimed, "*Die voeltjies van die hemel het hulle gatte op ons gedraai,*" (the angels of heaven have turned their arses on us) whilst thrusting her hand dramatically through a window pane, shattering the glass. I was the Spawn of the Devil.

My ancestral family originally went to South Africa due to religious persecution. There is a mystery behind what religion they actually were, and how or why they were persecuted. My mother thought that there might be some Jewish connection, but from what I know of them, they were probably intelligent Free Thinkers. Many people went to SA and New World countries because they felt that class and religious racism was wrong. Many, like my family, settled in Franschoek, which was a large settlement of French Huguenots who developed the wine industry. They built a beautiful monument to Religious Freedom and were educated, cultured and progressive. My great-grandfather was famous for his progressive ideas, nature-friendly farming methods and insistence on equality. He built houses for and educated the mixed-race workers on the Estate which was very unusual at the time. He was a human engineer who was very popular and liked. My great-grandmother was a talented pianist who could have performed at concert level. Musicality runs in the family.

My grandfather had to move up to the Transvaal to do his engineering work and life there was very different. Despite the Protestant breakaway, the Dutch Reformed community in Johannesburg was conservative and restrictive, particularly towards women, children and people of colour. White men were all-powerful demigods. Revolution became Institution.

My mother wanted to defect to the Catholic Church as some form of misguided 'out of the frying pan into the fire' rebellion against this. I was eventually christened when I was four years old at a Catholic Church in Pretoria. I was named after Saint Dennis and Saint Stephen.

After my parents married we went to church a few times but that was an Anglican Church. Those visits faded out and we never went to church as a family again.

In the Wings

This is the Apartheid Regime society they were born into:

Tom	New Dutch Reformed (Rebels who rebel against the rebels.) *Broederbond* (Brother Bond sexist racists)	Conservative Racist Sexist Chauvinist hypocrites who unfortunately didn't seem to understand the essence of what Jesus was on about	Rebelled
Mary	Dutch Reformed (Original rebels) Racist and Chauvinist	Conservative Racist Sexist Chauvinist Hypocrites who unfortunately didn't seem to understand the essence of what Jesus was on about	Rebelled

They were joined in rebellion against this strange Apartheid Christianity, but were too damaged and lost their way despite their good intentions. The 'road to hell' and all that jazz...

Revolution turned into Institution again... and became an evil dictatorship.

And as I survived my home regime, battered by the storms of life, I resolved to learn to read and write as fast as I could, so that I could learn about life and one day I could write my story. So that one day I would be able to speak up about the unfairness, and the millions of victims like me… and the world would listen…

At the age of five I knew that I had something to say.

But in the meantime I would be a pretty and useful object. I was photographed by a top world photographer for a carpet advert. Pink tights and make-up hid my bruises, and a smile hid the pain in my heart. A quiet little girl with a lot to say and the despairing thought: Who will ever listen to me?

Maybe in 2012 the world would be ready? Ready for a Fair World Order?

STARTING AGAIN IN SCOTLAND

The years leading to 2012...

When I moved to the UK in 2007 I was very excited to join the First World. The First World Countries sell themselves so well internationally. Especially the UK and America. Their global marketing is impeccable. They are seen to be the countries who care about democracy and all injustices. Their news is the world's news. If some old lady in Skye farts in church – the whole world knows about it. Perfect! I thought. Finally ears will listen. Before we left South Africa I thought to myself: Universities are the places that foster the most progressive thought and activism. So as soon as we had settled I signed up for courses at a couple of universities. Finally I would get the support I was looking for... Huh! There was a good mix of being exploited and ignored by people who can't handle the realities of life. But that is another story and I am not going to go into it right now. All I will say is that I found myself itching to moon certain lecturers, which goes strongly against my usual ladylike disposition!

Jasmine Rose:

Ha ha! The word Professor is probably an etymological derivative of 'f-ing Oppressor'!

I agree with Martha Beck, who wrote the book *Expecting Adam*, when it comes to Academia and her IQ vs EQ stance. But I have to admit that there was good stuff too. There is potential for a truly positive academic experience - if only we could slow down the Rat Race.

I did thoroughly enjoy my Screenwriting Course. Film has been an escape for me since I was a little girl. Thank goodness for all those trips to the Drive-in. They saved my sanity. They gave me permission, together with my books, to lose myself in the land of fantasy – and to find answers to life. Good screenwriters who raise and reflect life issues are the unproclaimed Yodas of this planet and deserve far more respect and recognition than they get. I had planned on doing a creative writing course to help with writing this book, but the times didn't work out. So I found myself studying the exciting art of Changing the World through Visual Images.

I will share with you some of my first puny attempts:

My first screenwriting assignment was to write a scene with a lecturer and student: The lecturer was to be concerned at the tardiness of his student and confront the issue in a one–on-one scene of dialogue. The Screenwriting lecturer (I shall call him Duncan MacDougal) offered himself as a character, saying that it would be easier to write about a real person for our first attempt. He said that we should try to 'get' him and his character as part of the exercise... brave man.

I sat in *Ecco Vino* in Cockburn Street and started writing something very worthy about the student having to support a paralysed family member, but then looked wryly up at the darkening skies and allowed myself to go off on a tangent...

In the Wings

WEATHER REPORT - *BASED ON TRUE WEATHER...*

EXT. EDINBURGH UNIVERSITY - DAY

A dour, gray, scratchy blanket of a day - the steady drizzle that dampens Buccleuch Place is broken by flashes of sharp, bright lightning. DUNCAN MCDOUGAL rushes energetically through the downpour. He is followed by an oblivious MICHAEL, his talented but tardy student. He is dragging his feet, head hanging wearily. He enters the lecture room and is unpleasantly surprised to see that Duncan is there already...

INT. LECTURE ROOM - DAY

>DUNCAN MCDOUGAL
>Michael! You are one of the most promising and talented students, but you are not doing the work. What is going on?

>MICHAEL
>Uhhh - you know... stuff?

>DUNCAN MCDOUGAL
>Sorry, no. I don't know. It's a crime to waste potential like yours. What is it? Is it a woman? Love stuff? Problem at home?

>MICHAEL
>Um well...thanks. It's kind of both.

>DUNCAN MCDOUGAL
>You always look run ragged. You used to be together. What happened?

>MICHAEL
>You wouldn't believe me...

Flash into Michael's memory: A blonde, Charlize Theron look-alike is seen - naked, chest heaving, triumphantly dominating Michael as she rides him passionately. Dark clouds and bright lightning behind her, creating a halo of her blonde hair. Any man's dream.

>DUNCAN MCDOUGAL
>I'm a writer. I know that truth is stranger than fiction.

(CONTINUED)

CONTINUED:

> MICHAEL
> Okay... You know the Scottish weather and how crap it is?

> DUNCAN MCDOUGAL
> Oh - you suffer from Seasonal Affective Disorder?

Michael collapses on a chair

> MICHAEL
> No, not really - it's something else...I'm shagged out!
>
> It's Alien women who hide their space ships behind gray clouds. They have been trying to repopulate their planet with earth studs for centuries! They have low fertility and the men died out. Scottish males who have been disciplined, de-chauvinized and de-caved are their ideal specimens! The phallic loch legend gets them going...They all look like film stars and come for me at night. They pay with gold coins from their bellies! I need the money - och it's hard to say nay...

Flash into both their minds: blonde, brunette and redhead bombshells belly dancing suggestively - gold sparkling and dripping from their navels.

> DUNCAN MCDOUGAL
> But what about the nice days?

> MICHAEL
> The good days are their monthlies!

Duncan gazes transfixed.
> (BEAT)

> DUNCAN MCDOUGAL
> So the few sunny days are Alien's periods... and these gorgeous women put in a lot of work to get fertilized?

> MICHAEL
> Aye.

Duncan paces, rubbing palms energetically, exuding pent up excitement, building gradually to a gleeful grin.

(CONTINUED)

CONTINUED:

>   DUNCAN MCDOUGAL
>   Wow - whole new angle on
>   relationship dynamics. Boy gets
>   girl thrown on it's head...
>   Mmm... As you know the well-being
>   of my students comes first...
>
>   So I will share the coins and take
>   your place!

Well, somebody had to come up with an entertaining theory on the weather to stop the SAD hoards from flinging themselves off the various castle ramparts... Great Porno Plot potential!

Humour has always helped me adjust to difficult circumstances.

Chapter 3

Exodus into the Wilderness

Afrikaans saying: *Hulle doen alles gatkantvoer*

Direct Translation: They do everything arse-ways/back-to-front

STARTING AGAIN IN SCOTLAND - TRAVELS

Rockville Hotel by the Sea, Joppa Rocks, Portobello

I recommend Room Ten - nestled in the eaves right at the top, overlooking the sea and the rocks which are 300,000,000 years old.

The waves swish and sparkle,

A magical sound.

I am so high up in my little writing nook that I have the illusion of being in a lighthouse. The *Famous Five* and *Nancy Drew* were always having adventures in lighthouses...

I feel like the rocks and I are fellow ancients and friends. The water is my family.

They have to be as I have so few in Edinburgh.

Joppa is my home from home...

I come and write at the Rockville so often that I am almost part of the family.

(Well, 'the special needs member who lives in the attic', according to the hilarious owner.)

In the Wings

> Being in this place makes writing feel like an adventure, even though this is a hard tale to tell.
>
> A story from a lighthouse –
>
> To reverse the madness and shine a light to brighten the darkness in the world.

I danced for the first time on stage at the Johannesburg Dance Eisteddfod at age five. I was given the main role as the Fairy Queen in a sparkly silver and white tutu in the group dance, and also had a solo as a bright green worm. My parents worked hard on my costumes and created a giant red papier mâché apple for the 'worm' to pop out of.

Mary tried to be the perfect mother, but she was already well into her colluding role - creating the illusion to everyone that everything was okay. But it was not, and some very scary changes were being planned…

Tom devised the plan for us to move to Cape Town - away from any interfering or protecting family. This is what psychopaths do. They isolate their victims. Divide and conquer.

(According to Thomas Sheridan who wrote *Puzzling People: The Labyrinth of the Psychopath* the latest statistics for varying degrees of psychopathy is 1 in 22 people. This includes the narcissistic, sociopathic parasitic manipulators who find killing inconvenient. These are mostly men with women and children as their main victims. One out of every twenty two people you meet. This is a very important fact to know! When you know that, you know that stories like mine are common, not rare.

There are messed up people out there and we are all damaged by them.)

He sold Cape Town as the Land of Opportunity and Adventure as he puffed out yellow smoke and wove his magic on my mother. He made us follow his Dagga Dream. 'Drugs talking – must move'. Things in his body were moving. His teeth were already falling out in his mid-twenties because of the amount of LSD and Speed that he had taken and his brain was calcifying.

Jasmine Rose:(Erm. She gets a bit ranty and preachy…)

Drugs are not fun. They destroy bodies and brains. They are not recreation. They cause hell for families. And, no, Timothy Leary, McKenna and Co - they are not an important part of shamanism. Anyone who has done a real shamanic journey would know that. They may speed up the process but are definitely not essential – and even among tribal people drugs have a tendency to get out of hand. The resultant schizo and psychotic episodes are not fun. Yet another bloody thing that is sold as trendy and chic, as it makes us all sick!

The next major memory is of being on the train, rattling through the Karoo with all the worldly possessions somewhere in a crate. Initially we moved into a pleasant flat on the central peninsula and they both got jobs. My father as a crane driver at the harbour, and my mother worked in a Nursing Home. But then The Seventies Depression hit South Africa.

(Economic disasters spell domestic disaster, as women and children become the main targets for male frustration: Men mess up economy. Men fired and at home getting up to crap. Domestic and child abuse figures sky-rocket. The men at the top cut funding for aid organizations. Children become economical, disease-free sex and violence targets with little recourse for help. A cheap thrill.)

Tom was fired, in the 'last in first out' system. This was a huge blow to his ego. My mother was pregnant and now she was the only breadwinner. I was stuck at home with his mad, pent-up, frustrated energy. Every day was torture. He had his schemes and regimes that had to be carried out. His bored, addled mind had to find bizarre things to do to amuse itself.

Once he cut my food funding and starved me the whole day, then sent me to sleep in my room. My tummy was grumbling so I couldn't nod off, much as I wanted to escape my reality. He kept coming into the room to check whether I was sleeping or not, and I was so terrified that I would get a hiding if I wasn't, that of course, I couldn't sleep. I tried to pretend but that didn't work. I was shaking in fear. Every time he came in he would interrogate:

"Why aren't you asleep?" Eventually I said, "I'm too hot."

So he pulled all the blankets off me.

The next time I cried, "I'm too cold!"

He furiously brought all the blankets in the house and piled them on top of me - then the pillows and the carpets too. I was a tiny little five-year-old smothering under a mountain. I knew what it must feel like to be trapped under rubble in a disaster. I had nightmares and fears about that for years.

Eventually he gave me some water. But by this time I was so sick with nerves I threw it all up.

I remember his observational fascination, like I was an animal in an experiment. He asked bemusedly how I could throw up if I had nothing in my stomach?

And he laughed. I had succeeded in amusing him. He then went out and said that he would bring me some sweets if I slept while he was away. I did eventually pass out from sheer relief and exhaustion. When he came back he brought me liquorice... which I hated.

What was that whole episode about? Needing to get out for drugs I suppose, but he didn't do that again. He went back to his habit of taking me with him to carry the 'groceries'. Forced to be a criminal at age five and my mother was a criminal for allowing it.

By this stage the throwing up thing was very much part of my life. I was in such a state of nerves by the time my father came home at night that I would be nauseous. I was unused to the type of food that he liked - hot curries and exotic spicy foods which don't work for children - so my stomach would seize up. I would try to get to the toilet in time only to be screamed at and beaten with a thick leather belt. When I desperately tried to keep it in and not leave the room, I unavoidably threw up in my plate. Tom made to eat the food anyway... vomit and all. It tasted bad, but the degradation tasted worse.

Any action of mine could trigger off terrible punishing repercussions. He was training me to be his fearful slave. For example, even if my little girl tummy stuck out too much, he would punch and wind me, telling me to suck my stomach in. I lived on the permanent in-breath. I still do, and I suffer from organ pain. So many women - up to 80% in some areas - suffer Irritable Bowel Syndrome and ulcers from having to swallow continuous decades of abuse.

Thank goodness I had my sparkly silver and white tutu and crown. I would put them on and dance away the fear and agony. I would be the fairy princess and twirl, as I raised my wand and wished away the suffering in the world. It made me feel good.

But one night I was 'so bad' that Tom packed up my little suitcase with some clothes and threw me out. He marched me two blocks or so away from our flat to a deserted field. He had taken me out into the dark night away from my mother and any hope of protection.

My crime on this occasion was that I had painted mushrooms and fairies on the face bricks of the balcony. I had done it so beautifully and carefully. I had been left alone to play by myself while they had an 'afternoon nap'. I was desperate to find something that would win me some approval. As I listened to the symphony of their lovemaking, I thought it would please them if I showed that I loved them - maybe they would love me? I knew it would wash off if they didn't like it. They absolutely hated it.

I scrubbed it off with a brush and soap, but that wasn't enough... I was beaten with a thick leather belt, but according to Tom I wasn't sorry enough, because I tried to explain that I did it out of love, so the torture carried on into the night. He forced me to pack a few things into my little suitcase and he marched me out of the flat, away from my mother, neighbours and light and pushed me into a dark field.

On the pitch-black field he gave me the choice of 'having the hiding of my life' or leaving. I naturally chose to leave. I picked up my little suitcase and walked towards the bright lights of the main road. I was already planning ahead and had left him behind. I would go to the café where the nice Indian family were and I would ask them for help. Maybe I could live with them, or maybe they could help me find some good parents… maybe I could go back to my grandparents or my uncle… they loved me.

I felt totally shocked and betrayed as I was grabbed from my path to planned freedom and hauled backwards into the blackness again. Tom hit me, shook me and screamed, "Choose again!" Choice-less, I was duly dragged home for the hiding.

My mother's take on the whole event was rather odd. She would tell this as a funny family story explaining how she had to make my father sweet tea for shock, because I was so 'stubborn' that I had chosen to leave. Hilarious!

That night I was left to cry myself to sleep… without tea or love or comfort of any kind.

Mary had already told me that I had to do the British thing: Shut-up and stiff upper lip.

Jasmine Rose:

Betrayed by your own parents! How do you ever trust again after that?

So there: at the ripe old age of five you <u>DID</u> *choose to create something different – but you weren't allowed. It's fine for gurus to preach about 'choice', but women and children still have very little power of choice in the face of male domination. The worst are women who mindlessly preach the preachings. They betray and silence their sisters and daughters and destroy their choice even more*!

Carl Jung *said, "People will do anything not to face true evil".*

Armchair theories created to avoid having to do anything. It's total money-spinning and building power on the misery of others - colluding in indifference whilst peddling healing and promises of success. Maniacs! They are like Zambezi sharks. You think you are safe swimming in a freshwater river and next thing you have a shark biting your foot!

Obviously there are many people out there who consistently cause total disaster for themselves, but it is just plain stupid to say that you as an individual create EVERYTHING that happens to you. The sheer arrogance of it! It's like a surfer boasting that he managed to ride every wave. Sometimes we ride the wave and sometimes we get dumped! Or the shark gets us. All of us. No room for egos.

It was unusual that in the height of Apartheid, I, a little white girl, would have chosen to run to an Indian family. I had no sense of race because we were often in District 6 or one of the townships to get my father's drugs. Some of the biggest fighters against Apartheid in the white community were the people who wanted their drugs more accessible. One of the biggest changes they wanted in the new constitution was legalisation of drugs. Dodgy motives.

My parents were very tricky and hard to understand. They would profess to be racist but still mix, against the law and curfews - and actually did do some good work helping people in the townships. Very confusing and inconsistent. They were the rebels who had a knee-jerk reaction to champion the underdog, and oppose the person in power in any given situation. But they very clearly did not feel that the underdogs were equal to them.

Tom was also violently anti-gay on the one hand but could flirt and butter up when needed, so the homosexuals loved him and his 'eccentricity'. He understood their language and could speak it. Even the girls' names instead of words code language.

You may require more explanation of the South African Girls' Names Gay Code Language which will help give you more of an understanding of the SA theatre world:

So camp. Someone might say very gently: "Oh Sheila, I just made a Hilda Florrie!" Translated this means: "Oh shit, I just made a horrible fart." Sheila is shit and Hilda is horrible. It sounds so much prettier in code language. Maybe we should start a new trend on *Facebook*?

Here are some more words from the beautiful Gay Language:

Beulla = beautiful

Stella = steal

Nancy = no

Nora = nerd

Hilda = horrible

Wendy = white

Betty = black

Clora = coloured/mixed race

So here is another example sentence:

"Nancy Nora! That Hilda Clora who doesn't know whether she is a Betty or a Wendy, Stella-ed my Beulla eye pencil."

Which means: "No you nerd! That horrible mixed-race person who doesn't know whether she is going for black or white stole my beautiful eye pencil."

This is in fact a fairly typical sentence to hear, together with its racist and intelligence insults. It is a sin to be a 'try-for-white' according to all races. During Apartheid I was a white girl with olive-toned and tanned skin. I was often asked: "What are you?" and accused of being not quite white by all races. I was called a 'try-for-white'. I didn't fit into any of the boxes.

Jasmine Rose:

When will people understand that we are all just humans suffering the human condition on Earth. I wish some giant Mother would reach down and bang the heads together and scold: "Play nicely! You are all the same! Learn to share!"

Gawd Jeeves – the planet is such a small little rock in the sky. When will people think global?

The UK is little bits of land on a few small islands still at loggerheads with each other and with massive chips on the shoulder over past ills. Getting all uppity with each other over classes. Move on people! To citizens from bigger progressive countries all the snobby nationalistic racism and class fascism seems a tad trite and silly. Forget past pride. We have all been fucked over, oppressed, persecuted, colonized and disenfranchised at some point or another. Draw a line and do something different people!

Around that time we moved to a smallholding in an undeveloped area. There was a house on a piece of land that belonged to the council, but they seemed to have forgotten about it, so we lived there rent free for about three years. It was lovely to be in the nature, but the isolated position and lack of landlord or neighbours, made it possible for my father to continue his reign of terror totally unchecked. In all the years of my childhood we seldom had a phone. There was no way to call for help.

At this stage I occasionally regressed back to bed-wetting… one of the signs of abuse which usually brings more torture on the victim.

My poor mother was very heavily pregnant when we moved in but, being the only breadwinner, she had to wake up at 4:30 in the morning to catch the bus and train to get to work by seven in the morning, and she would get home after 9:00 at night. I was again left at his mercy. He would create 'interrogation sessions' very much like ones you would experience in a Nazi war camp. He was totally obsessed with Hitler, the Nazis, and the Italian Brown Shirts. He wore brown clothes and forced us to also wear his uniform. (Very enjoyable for a little ballerina girl as you can imagine. I absolutely hated it and longed for colours.) He even painted some of the walls in the house brown. He devoured countless books about them, and the torture sessions were a way of indulging his fantasies.

It would go something like this:

T: Where is your fucking jersey?

D: I don't know.

(Punch in the arm)

T: How can you not know where your jersey is? How fucking old are you?

D: F-four.

T: Liar! You've just turned five!

(Slap across the face)

Go to your room and find your jersey. If you don't fucking find it I'm going to give you a hiding with the belt.

(Smack against the back of the head)

Five minutes later…

T: Hey fuckface - have you found it yet?

D: Which jersey? (Having been too scared and overwhelmed and in pain to ask up until now)

T: The fucking brown one you dumb cunt.

(Punch in the leg)

D: It's in the washing basket.

T: Why didn't you fucking say so in the first place. You just want to fuck around and waste my time, you little bitch! Get to the bathroom! Now I'm really going to give you the hiding of your life.

(Slap against the head)

Pull your pants down and bend over the bath. Stretch your fucking arms and stay there.

(Whack with the thick leather belt, so hard that I fall over)

T: Get up you shit! Bend! If you fall over again I'm going to hit you twice as hard!

(The hiding continues until he has had enough…)

I am crying in utter despair of pain, humiliation, hopelessness…

T: Shut the fuck up! If you cry any more I'm going to give you another hiding! Get to your fucking room and stay there!

This is a very shortened version. It usually played itself out over at least two or three hours.

I was so well trained to stop crying instantly, despite pain and sadness.

I can remember enduring a session like that, and then trying to stop crying as he commanded. But I was still hiccupping as children do when they have had a really bad shock - only to be sent right back for another hiding for 'fucking hiccupping'.

At times one of these 'interrogation sessions' would happen daily. Or I would be pulled out of my bed and woken up in the middle of the night to be punished for some fabricated wrongdoing.

But the worst was when my mother worked night duty, and he would wake me at about 5:30 in the morning to lie in bed with him and watch Venus fading and the sun rising, while he fiddled and fondled and told me how much he loved me.

He sang a song about sunshine and how I made him happy in grey weather.

Charity Galas:

One of the biggest joys for me as a professional dancer was the Charity Gala Evenings. It was such a great feeling to know that we were creating a wonderful magical evening for people where they could dress up and wear bling and feel good about raising money for an important cause, like suffering children.

That is the great, unrecognized work that us dancers do. In Africa, dancers have done protest theatre, outreach projects during Apartheid and helped feed millions. We have taken Education Shows to the smallest mud hut villages and brought joy and a moment of brightness and beauty to many.

One Gala Event stands out in my mind...

We performed Swan Lake *and then had a super-quick change into fishnets and high heels to do a showgirl high-kicking number. (For some reason the audiences always took great delight in seeing the ballerinas demoted to show girlies.)*

We had been practising for weeks with our top hats. The routine was slick and smooth. The choreographer was a hard task master and we dared not mess up!

Unfortunately the hot ice condensation in the misty final act of Swan Lake *had made the floor slick and smooth too! As we made our entrance, running in our heels, the first girls slid-teetered- tottered-slipped and smacked down – ungracefully - onto their derrières.*

'One – bang! – two - crash! - singular sensation every little step you take!'

It was certainly sensational. Luckily I was fourth in line so I had some warning and managed to keep to my feet. We were all completely rattled and everyone lost steps somewhere along the line. That must have been one of the worst Gala Evening Showgirl performances ever!

Ha ha! The audience loved it though. Nothing is as delightful as seeing an uppity ballerina fall on her arse - and the sympathy money for the cause rolled in.

During my first week at school my brother was born. It was a blustery, stormy day with gale force winds roaring across the Cape peninsula. The 'Black South-Easter' broke a number of windows in the hospital.

The birth was difficult and stormy too. My mother had to get my father to leave because he wanted to beat up the doctor. How terrible it must have been. Labour is hard enough without still having to break up a fight in the middle of it! My brother was very overdue and the cord was around his neck, but finally and reluctantly he made his way into this world. I've always felt that my brother had a death wish from before he was even born. In the last months of the pregnancy he must have heard the screaming, shouting, swearing and crying. He must have felt the adrenalin and fear in my mother's body and felt how it affected the development in his. The world could not have felt very enticing at all. He must have then already felt disempowered to help his sister or mother… to do anything about their abuse and tears. He must have felt rage and probably already decided then that he 'didn't want to know'.

(Modern neuroscience has proven that brain development is altered to create exactly this effect in children within domestic abuse environments and their memory system is damaged as a form of self-preservation.)

The really unfair thing for me is that by the time my brother was about five or so things calmed down a little in terms of violence because my father had by then been reported to the police, and his energies were moving much more into the sexual sphere and the secret molesting. So he has little or no conscious memory of the really horrible physical tortures that were being performed on me and our mother. That is what can really drive me mad sometimes and make me feel completely isolated. My father put that psychopathic curse on me very successfully. Keep the victim isolated... manipulate all situations so that no-one will believe her or listen – even the direct witnesses.

My poor brother, Seton, had a big trip laid on him about his birth. About the stormy weather and that he nearly died due to being overdue, and the cord being around his neck like the demonic boy in one of the horror movies. He hated his name and hated himself a lot. My father would call him Satan or Swine or *Sweinhund*. Tom acted out all his stuff on my poor brother. Tom felt cursed from the day he was born and he made damn sure that he passed that onto Seton and me.

My brother was my baby. I was so protective of him. I spent hours looking after him, feeding him, walking up and down with him cuddled in my arms to put him to sleep. In fact I think he was confused about who his mother really was. Mary had to go back to work as soon as possible and so a lot of the responsibility of looking after my brother came to me.

It's amazing when I think of it. There I was, this undersized little six-year-old nurturing the baby, walking back-breakingly up and down rocking him to sleep. Now that I have been a mother myself and see how much work it is, I really don't know how I did it.

In the first year of Seton's life my father was supposed to be looking after the baby and studying to pass his matric exams which he had missed out on, but he faded on that. He spent his time getting high, sleeping and making me do things around the house, or ordering me to 'keep the little shit quiet'. So much for the house-husband theory.

I was constantly worried about feeding Seton, and any pocket money I received, or money that I was given by people, I would save in my orange piggy bank so that when money ran out at the end of the month, there would be back-up for bread and milk. We were so poor (like they say in the classics) that we would sometimes have to sell the clothes off our back at the Squatter Camp up the road. The children in the Squatter Camp and townships seemed richer and happier than me. Life felt upside-down.

But everything in that Regime felt topsy-turvy. I recall thinking in my childlike way, why are the lots of people being bossed by the few people in their own land? They need someone to teach them logical sense! But who would listen? I looked at newspapers and tried to write my own. I was disturbed by the pictures of riots, torture and 'necklacing'. Why were the wrong people in charge? And why were the protestors killing each other by burning on tyres? It didn't make sense.

I pondered life. During holidays or after school, we used to go to work with my mother, and I would dance and perform for the patients. I would chatter to them and enjoy helping with their comfort and take their minds off their pain for a brief while. The old ladies especially would often reward me with money. I loved doing it and it gave me great joy, but my family relied quite heavily at times on that income from my early community work. I learnt so much from the people in the homes. One lady had a great philosophy on cleanliness. She said the three essentials were the 'Three Fs':

Face, Feet and Fanny – and she demonstrated her theory with alacrity and a facecloth.

One year we created a magical fairy kingdom in a hospital room that brought joy to the children's ward and a magazine came to take pictures because it was so beautiful. My mother was a great artist, among all her other talents. The Angel with the demon. What a waste.

Tom eventually got a job as a technician at the *Cape Town Theatre*. The hours were long, and it was a great blessing that we saw a lot less of him. But working didn't seem to lessen his aggressive behaviour much. He would come home after a frustrating day and take it out on us.

Jasmine Rose:

As they do. Because they can.

One night my mother didn't want to go into the bathroom to run him a bath because there was a big spider in the bathroom. (No, running water was not something a Sultan did for himself.)

Often Tom would find her arachnophobia amusing, and would want to feel like the hero for removing the spider whilst belittling her. But this time he swore at her and forced her to go in.

She was screaming and crying and pleading, as he slapped her around and then threw her out of the house.

We lived in the middle of nowhere on wild land. There were millions of spiders, scorpions and snakes outside. She was weeping and begging to be let in at two in the morning.

I was terrified, all alone in my room. I was dying inside... not being able to help my mother and so afraid that she would leave and desert us, abandoning us with this monster. I don't remember whether my brother woke up or not.

I eventually needed the toilet desperately, but was too terrified to leave the room, so I was forced to crouch in the corner behind the *Dolly-Varden* dresser and released a puddle of urine. Like a small terrified animal in a cage. It was not the first or last time that this happened. I felt so ashamed but there was nothing else I could do. I thought, "I am like an animal."

Children feel the pain of degradation as much as adults – and they remember.

As do animals. We had a cat and it ran away after he hit it. We had a dog that ran away because he beat it with a belt. Fighting machines don't care who they hurt. I envied the animals that could run away so easily.

What a blessing that he was away more, but my mother had to stay up and cook him supper when he came in at 1:00am after a show – then be up again early for work to spend long hours on her feet caring for others at the hospital.

I don't know how she survived.

Jasmine Rose:

In the Wings

I don't know how most women survive. We are always doing too much for ungrateful wretches who use us in any way they can. And then they have the infernal cheek to project themselves onto us constantly, and are in defensive fear of the fact that a few of us may occasionally work out a way to use THEM!

I am sure that you are starting to sense that Jasmine is a ranting feminist. But she is the new wave of feminist. She doesn't want to be a man or be equal to one. She just wants fairness and to be her fabulous feminine self - to be respected and valued for that.

Jasmine Rose:

We all secretly know that we are better than them. The ladies who survive their spouses and gang up in retirement homes are very clear on the subject. They have lived a full life, produced and raised kids - and babied and buried their men. They know this truth for sure. The real 'Con of man' is that we are painted as the inferior little helpmates of men. If you look at the design it is clear that we are the main powerhouses who bring in and raise life, and men are supposed to be OUR helpmates. We are the miracle workers!

It has been scientifically proven that we are 3% more intelligent on average, more wise and better at learning tasks too. We are simply better people. So I am not interested in being like them, since it is clear that women rock!

You know what? I am a FAIRinist. I would settle for being treated like I am an equal human, not subhuman subspecies.

Denise Stephani

I grew up in a home where 'fuck' was fine, but 'feminism' and 'women empowerment' were dirty words. But I have always been uncomfortable with feminism simply because by rights it shouldn't even need to exist. It's mad that women still have to fight to be considered equal. Despite my personal disempowered circumstances, I never understood what the 'shaved-head, hairy armpit old feminist lezzer trouts' were on about. I didn't know what they meant, complaining about the 'keep her barefoot and pregnant in the kitchen' and 'slavery in marriage' issues, until I experienced it in my own relationships with 'New Men'. I thought it was only my father that was so crazy, and that it had all changed - but no. It merely changed form. 'New men' simply use new tactics to get sex and slaves.

Jasmine Rose:

Feminism has backfired on us. We need to worry about dying of underpaid exhaustion now from ALL the roles we have to take on. Women love to dance, but there is so little time for that now.

Now our 'partners' exhaust us and keep us powerless with pregnancy, children, housework AND career. Being only a housewife to 'do' for them is not good enough: now they all want a laying hen too. And governments want their double-income taxes.

Ha! But the manne *still feel entitled to spout rubbish like this:*

'Feminism encourages women to leave their husbands, kill their children, practise witchcraft, destroy capitalism and become lesbians.'

PATRICK ROBERTSON, US POLITICIAN 1992

denisestephani@god: Is 'female' a euphemism for 'floor mat'?

DENISE DOES DANCE FILM:

Here is my first attempt at a short film project involving dance. It got some good comments, like 'visual' and 'timeous piece of contemporary writing'. It also got called 'political' and 'leaning towards prose' in places. But hey – I'm a bookworm social reformer writing as such. What do you expect? It's hard to write about a Rwandan Genocide refugee without involving politics even if one is trying to do a lighter piece with humour and the odd boogie...

Jasmine Rose:

Urgh, weesht. Those wee boys in the film industry are so scared of 'preachiness'. The world could do with a bit of sensible preachiness right now! Not to mention a healthy bit of man-bashing...

It is based on the true story of the 14-year-old teenager, Valentina, who survived the Rwandan Genocide but the location is moved to Scotland with her settling as an asylum seeker in the UK. The school, social setting and issues reflect true experiences that I had teaching in the community in Scotland.

4 THOSE WHO NEVER MADE IT

EXT.BUSY STREET EDINBURGH - DAY

It is not the chocolate brown of VALENTINA's skin that makes her stand out in the British crowd. It is the intensity in the eyes of the 14 year-old Rwandan refugee, as she gazes forward with complete focus. One bright red glove covers a mutilated hand with fingers missing.

She is at the edge of a busy road - rising on the toes of one foot only, her other leg extended behind her, in a low arabesque. She is testing her balance against the madness and chaos of the early morning traffic.

EXT. VALENTINA'S ANIMATED MAGIC LAND - DAY

Her mind is miles away as she sees herself as a Ninja-style warrior princess... improving her fighting skills by challenging her will on the edge of a cliff in a magical land.

EXT.BUSY STREET - DAY

As the traffic lights change, she glides forward, free and floating. Valentina shines in the tight, closed crowd.

She is wearing a MP3 player and earphones. She dances and weaves through the busy throng - mouthing the words to the funky African beat.

BACKGROUND MUSIC :

> VALENTINA
> I wish it was Friday, Friday...
> life is stressing me out... Does
> any soul get me?

A boy moves away from the wall, zipping up, and she is forced to throw herself into a jump, flying over a puddle of fresh piss - to enter the school yard. She arrives at the same time as SUSAN GRAY the dowdy school secretary who hurries, head down, to her office.

EXT. SCHOOL YARD - DAY

(CONTINUED)

In the Wings

CONTINUED:

Rough, dirty, dysfunctional - a co-ed school that takes in "Youth at Risk" for funding reasons, but doesn't know what to do with them. The halls echo with Asbo bait. It smells of gangs, date rape and drugs.

As she crosses the schoolyard Valentina leaps like a Springbok to avoid slipping on a used condom - and a scattered marble game.

EXT. VALENTINA'S (ANIMATED) MAGICAL LAND - NIGHT

The condom becomes a magical hot air balloon floating up into the galaxies - the marbles are stars and worlds below her...

INT. SCHOOL - DAY

She goes through the main doors and dodges. She manoevres a side slide - and avoids the school bullies grabbing victims for drug money.

She runs down the school corridor SCREECHING to a halt with an 'attitude' street-pose freeze - right in front of her friend MORAG. They LAUGH linking arms and enter the classroom together.

INT. CLASSROOM - DAY

Valentina grabs Morag's hand twirls her and pushes her into her seat, then sits, her FRIDAY THEME MUSIC ending on a SCREECHING DJ DRAG as a boy roughly pulls out her earphones.

Various mutterings from:

                   CLASSMATES
     Posh cow... She's not posh - she's
     a chav dumb African... Didn't you
     read what we wrote on Bebo?
     Pirouette back to Africa black
     shite...Britain is for Brits,
     prancing fairy fuck.

Valentina is recording the scene on her mobile.

                   CLASSMATES
     Chuck that old rubbish mobile!

A teacher enters SHOUTING abuse - ending the hostilities - but O.S. we still hear a girls' cat fight MEOUW-RING in the hall.

Chapter 4

The Attractive Overactive Imagination

Afrikaans saying: *Hy maak my deurmekaar*

Translation: He makes me messed-up (confused).

'The world is not dangerous because of those who do harm, but because of those who look at it without doing anything." Albert Einstein

STARTING AGAIN IN SCOTLAND

Scotland: Burntisland & Aberdour

Every time I travel through Aberdour on my way to Forth View or Burntisland in Fife, I pass the castle and misread the bakery sign. It is called *C. Lonie* but every time I see the word 'Colonic' and expect to witness people staggering out bow-legged, pained, but lighter in the bowel region.

My mental aberration may have something to do with the fact that the spooky and intriguing *Green Witch* shop is just along from it, so there is the expectation of a town littered with esoteric happenings.

I love those funny little life things.

Humour helps well-being despite life trials.

I started a joke and riddle book when I was eight and collected humour. I used to roll around laughing at the *Reader's Digest* 'Laughter is the Best Medicine' jokes, instinctively finding the things that help to heal.

Scotland loves its comedians.

In the Wings

Here is a good saying send-up I found in the Ladies toilets at *Tir Nir Nagog Centre* near Loch Lomond the other day:

> 'You come into this world alone and naked, you get slapped on the arse...
>
> And then things get worse!'

Good thing that I could see the funny side of being stuck with a torturing homicidal maniac...

I threw myself into my school activities and my dancing. There was a dance teacher at the school so I could finally resume lessons. I did very well and passed an RAD exam with Honours. Every week I went home with gold stars plastered in my little star book.

I was challenged to dance the Butterfly Dance particularly magically. Tom insisted that my scarf wings attached to my back should be a dull moth brown colour. I had to make my personality sparkle and create colourful magical worlds with my body to overcome that bit of meanness.

I found the joy anyway.

But straight after, I was rushed home from ballet and parked on a chair at the kitchen basin to wash the dishes in boiling hot water. The skin on my hands looked old and wrinkled from the burns. More torture for my skin. I had to clean the brown carpet on my hands and knees, and wipe the newly painted brown walls that my brother had messed on. I had to listen to the exploits of the Nazis and the Italian Brown Shirts that Tom was obsessed with. He would read out grizzly facts and show pictures of concentration camps and torture. He justified their terrible actions. He went a step beyond Holocaust Denial. He said that it was a good thing because the Jews were 'asking for it' and had 'brought it on themselves'. He said that the British were hypocrites because they had started the concentration camp system first. They had test-driven the concentration camp model in South Africa and starved thousands of women and children to death during the Anglo-Boer war. (This is true, actually.) He would expound on his theories to other people too, and they would nod in agreement. It is amazing how quickly and easily psychopathic actions are condoned and glorified in this world.

I was living in brown smudgy darkness. He said that people over 60 were 'oxygen thieves' and should be put down. He said that many people were Zombies without souls. I had to work hard to keep myself in the light. I played with my angelic little brother, danced, and spent as much time as I could in nature. I would plant seeds and watch them grow and I would try to communicate with the birds.

I played in my imagination, lying on my back, watching magical kingdoms unfold in the Cloud Theatre up in the bright blue African skies. When we went to movies at the Drive-in Theatre I lost myself deep inside them. Even the scary inappropriate ones I was taken to see, like *Clockwork Orange*, *The Twisted Nerve*, *Suspiria* and *Tommy*. They gave me nightmares because they were a very real reflection of what I was dealing with.

(Since my father came into my life I have been plagued by anxiety nightmares – and a recurring one about being bitten by snakes. Horrible. I wake up shaking and sweating, with painful pins and needles all over my body. So no real respite even in sleep. I have had to work very hard at developing coping strategies.)

In the Wings

Thank goodness he also liked humour and action, so we saw Bud Spencer and Terence Hill movies, *Pink Panther*, *The Duchess and the Dirtwater Fox*, the *Carry On* films and *James Bond*. *Mad Magazines* featured in the home and we listened to Spike Milligan, *Just a Minute* and *The Goons*.

I painted and drew fairies, butterflies, flowers, mushrooms and hobbits. I drew the mushrooms, red ones with white spots, and hobbits, because my father liked it. He said that he was like a hobbit, and hobbits like *Amanita Muscaria* mushrooms which make you see hallucinations and 'give you mind expansion'.

My school reports, although not bad, were a reflection of what was going on: 'Denise must stop daydreaming in class', 'Denise must attend school more regularly' but nobody seemed to notice… One school report triggered off major disaster for me:

'Denise must talk less in class'.

I hadn't yet quite cottoned onto the old school class dynamic of being quiet and giving the teacher the floor.

The triggered nightmare event brought about three very important realisations:

1) My father was mad and beyond logic… and that he was the one who was wrong.

2) There was something wrong with my mother too.

(These are crucial realisations in recovering from an abuse childhood. It is the children who never reach these conclusions who suffer the most, and go off the rails.)

3) I was to be silent and cover up for them.

On this day Tom arrived early to pick us up from my mother's work. I have a feeling it was his intention to 'check up on us'. At the time Mary was playing with the idea of leaving him and had been in contact with a nursing council lawyer. I don't think he was aware of that fact, but he was insanely jealous. He was concerned that someone might chat my mother up, that she would find her common sense, and leave him.

He, like many mad people, had strong intuitions as well as neurosis, and he was probably sensing something. So it wasn't just a psycho that I was dealing with but a psychic too! Do you know how tough that was to deal with? Psychopaths are excellent at reading people, but he could definitely sometimes read minds too. He loved people-watching and could pick up on their thoughts in a rather scary manner. The African people were convinced that he was a *Sangoma* (witch doctor) and were very careful around him. His childhood of having to survive would have heightened his senses and observation skills, as it has heightened mine. He often spoke about how he had developed his mind power. This development of hyper-vigilance for survival became useful for manipulation and abuse of power.

So that is the mood in which he arrived at her work - angry and psychically sensing.

I was walking in the grounds of the hospital with two friends and a bag of sweets. I was sometimes allowed sweets, when he wanted to manipulate me, but at other times not. Although I hid the sweets he somehow knew I had them. This became a day on which I was not allowed. He glared at me growling that he would "see to me later". I was frantic, knowing by now what to expect, so I threw

In the Wings

the sweets away in the bin hoping that this action would save me. It didn't help at all.

All the way home I was punched in the legs, slapped and terrorized as he swerved and careered the car about the roads. So the near-death fear of dying in a car accident was added on top of the pile of trauma.

I told him that I had thrown the sweets away but he screamed that I was a liar, and that now I was "going to get two fucking belt hidings - one for the sweets and one for the lying."

He threw me into the bathroom and beat me till I lay a quivering, snivelling ball, on the floor. Then made me stand in front of him, while he lay on his bed rolling cigarettes, smoking and interrogating me, repeating that I was a liar and the real hiding was still coming. He had a *Pixar* spotlight-type lamp next to his bed. He aimed the spotlight right in my face so that I was blinded.

Just like a Gestapo interrogation session.

I had no supper and I was knocked down and shoved into the bathroom to be beaten a few more times. I was so confused that I didn't know what to say because whatever I said, he seemed to find some angle or way to twist that into an extra offence. He wouldn't let me sit, or eat or wee.

I had no human rights. Or animal rights.

This carried on for hours on end into the night. I imagined myself away – far out of my body in some other land. He repeatedly back-handed me in the mouth till my lips were swollen, bleeding and blue, and he ranted on about lying and how bad I was.

My mother lay frozen in the bed and watched. She did nothing to protect or comfort me.

Eventually I was locked in my room and allowed to drift off into the blessing of sleep.

The next day I was in no condition to go to school. Questions would most certainly be asked as to why I was so battered, swollen and bruised.

A few days passed and eventually he took me back. All the way in the car he 'trained' me in what I must tell the teachers. He told me that I must say I was in a car accident. He punched me repeatedly in the legs till they were lame - till I got the story right. After all - a few more bruises would just add authenticity to the story. Today it was okay to lie. I didn't know the words for it, but I knew then, beyond any doubt, that he was an insane hypocrite. He set me up to be a liar in front of my mother so that she would never believe me again, but now he wanted me to lie for him!

Shortly after that I spoke to my mother and asked her if his behaviour was wrong. She said that I was naughty and should "count myself lucky because other parents put cigarettes out on their children's tongues and hands."

I hope that you GET how that made it all ten times worse and rubbed salt in the wound. Apart from that, it made her an accomplice and perpetrator too. Not just a silent witness.

When I was about seven, she was studying psychology, and she told me that he was a psychopath, because he knew how to hurt in a premeditated way so that he would get away with it. But she said that she loved him and she couldn't admit to her parents that they were right about him. She brought out those old chestnuts:

"I made my bed now I must lie in it."

"We can't wash our dirty laundry in public."

She also explained that if we spoke up we would not be safe – because humans behave like chickens. If they see a wounded chicken they will gather around and peck it to death, so therefore one can't show vulnerability. (Lots of truth in this last one, sadly. I hope that the readers of this book will prove that theory wrong.) I had to be her counsellor and comfort her when she cried, but she simply denied my reality.

Tom	Violent Child Abuser	Psychopath	Insane Manipulator
Mary	Accomplice who enabled and did nothing to help her child. Adopted mad behaviour herself	Knew she was married to a psychopath but did nothing about it	Allowed herself and her daughter to be manipulated, used and abused in an insane manner

Romeo and Juliet, State Theatre, Pretoria

Aah - the greatest love story of all time: self-righteous youth in luuurve, fighting against the closed-minded parents stuck in their rightness... community dysfunction put on display and the demise of young lovers who insist on being together against all odds. A beautiful ballet. One of my favourites, because of the wonderful music.

I'm not sure whether William Shakespeare should be praised, or dragged out into the village square and shot. My parents certainly saw themselves as Romeo and Juliet, the star-crossed lovers against family and community. I'm sure Shakespeare meant it as a warning for all, but humanity is complicated and tends to imitate stupidity in plays and films, instead of learning from it. Monkey see, monkey do. The 'does art imitate life, or life imitate art?' debate.

I had a silly moment in the ballet:

There was an ultra-quick change in the wings for some of the corps de ballet, *from fighting villager scene to Grand Lady at the Capulet Ball. Funny how the technicians and male dancers seemed to gather on that side of the stage around that time... There was always a quick flash of tits to be seen.*

It was touch and go whether the first people to make the entrance would make it in time (me and my gent partner) One performance a few fastenings wouldn't work and I was in a bit of a panic, but as the first booming dramatic Tchaikovsky ballroom dance chords started:

Oooompah, ooompah! Dumterum derumterum terum tertum ter-rumtum!

Me and my partner, noses stuck in the air - my hand placed on his in a ladylike manner - made our stately entrance from the first wing at the stage front. Embodying nobility, our bearing was proud, our posture was good.

(Despite struggling to keep on the heavy headdress, and not trip over the long dress and train)

Only problem was... I was proudly dragging a hanger and a pointe *shoe in my wake!*

Blissfully unaware I paraded through the Ball Entrance way, leaving my deposit centre stage, where Romeo and Mercutio removed the hanger and shoe, whilst manfully trying to make it look like it was all part of the story.

Ha ha! Love it when you get the principal male dancers working for you!

Life arrangements became scrambled after that. The idea was to head closer to the theatre where my father worked. This would save him the journey and struggle with the car which always broke down.

It is amazing how the universe reflects things back through inanimate objects. My father never had a car that worked properly for longer than a month or two. 'Car' is short for Karma. As a child I was convinced that the constant car problems were somehow connected to the breakdown in the family, and now that I have studied more about quantum mechanics and metaphysics, I am even more sure. It works according to the 'laws of attraction' and all that jazz - but how very cruel that an already stressed-out child had to deal with universal backlash too. It felt like I spent my life push-starting cars.

On a more practical mechanical note - he was definitely very hard on the cars. He would drive like a road rage maniac, taking out his moods on the car and the fellow road users. He enjoyed the terror of his passengers who were slapped if they dared to show their fear.

I was an unwilling witness and participant in many a chase, where he pushed drivers off the road and hit them for 'driving like fucking idiots'. Just dealing with his constant road rage was scarring enough. He felt that he was the 'king of the road' and nobody else knew how to drive. It was his mission to tutor them aggressively on the finer points of driving, punctuated by the mandatory slap across the face, or punch in the mouth.

He also had lots to say about karma. Whenever something unlucky happened he would say: "I must have been a bad person in my last life." Expecting sympathy from us, but also implying that the bad things that he was doing were our well-earned Karma! Yup – the paedos and abusers love quoting religious and spiritual texts to justify and aid their evil.

Once a driver he was bullying pulled a gun on us in retaliation – and Tom backed off, suddenly reasonable. Instant karma. I was dressed up and on the way to see the ballet. The outing, like so many others was completely ruined for me. I don't think I saw much of the ballet. My mind was in a numbed post-traumatic stress haze. One thing I do remember is that a very special ballerina was dancing. She was beautiful, blonde and lithe. I heard shortly after that she had landed up in an insane asylum. The combination of drugs, anorexia and the stress of the profession became too much for her.

I often think that the stress of the profession and the stress of my own life served to cancel each other out somewhat. Or at any rate, being at dancing was a relief for me, so I ignored much of the stress, bitching and problems of the dance world since it was mild compared to the stress, bitching and problems I had at home.

In the Wings

Jasmine Rose:

Why can't people just be nice? It takes up so much less energy. What's that thing they say?

It takes fourteen muscles to smile and 140 to frown? I want to start a Niceness Movement. I'll name it after you. De-nice, Be-nice! If the Horrible Humans supported and encouraged each other there would be more for everyone! Ben Elton wrote about it in his whodunit book Dead Famous:

'What we need is macrobiotic organic communities interacting with their environments in an atmosphere of mutual respect,' Woggle added.

'What the fahk are you talking about?' Garry enquired.

'Basically it would be nice if things were nicer.'

I wonder if sexy-minded Elton would be our first member to sign up for the Be-Nice Movement?

So no matter how ugly and competitive and soul-destroying it got in the ballet world, it was better than being at home. I guess if you are brought up on stress, a little more here or there makes very little difference - until, of course, it all catches up with you one day. I always thought that I was fine. I wasn't in denial, I had read the books, and I knew what was going on, so the nerves and depression wouldn't catch up with me. Ha! What a joke.

Jasmine Rose:

For goodness sake - dancing is supposed to be fun!

And I suppose when you try to tell your story everyone cuts you short and says to you:

"Don't live in the past", and "What doesn't kill you makes you strong". They push you into De-Nial and De-pression. Bet you want to De-lete all these unhelpful catchphrases that people fling at you...

Hello! What doesn't kill you causes years of pain, suffering, nightmares and problems for decades in your future. This is the side effect. Or direct effect. In many cases getting killed would be a blessing. Who the heck wants to stick around suffering and being 'strong'. It must also make you fearful, make so much in your life difficult...

Yes you're tough – but you live every day with the damage and consequences of that which nearly killed you! It's not quality of life.

I faced the threat of death every day. And tortures continued.

Another Tom favourite was making me lie in the sun until I burnt. Then he would make me get into a very hot bath and shove my head under water until I thought I would drown. My mother would tell him that cold water was better for burnt skin, but he was convinced that his method of 'healing' was superior. He was punishing my skin. My dark Mediterranean skin. The same as him. The same dark skin that caused his racist father to reject him. How many people are punished for the skin they're in?

The tortures continued and I went to school with colourful black and blue marks on my legs and body. I was ahead of the class in most subjects, so the obvious signs of abuse that teachers look out for which involve poor school performance were signs that were missing. I won the storytelling prize, and had my own reading group because I was reading books two years ahead of the rest of the class. I wanted to learn as much as I could, as fast as I could, so that I could read up on what was happening to me and work out what to do. I read my mother's psychology books and learnt about the factors which lead to abuse. We ticked all the boxes. I didn't have many friends. The other children thought I was a weird swot and teacher's pet with strange parents who dressed me funny.

I developed stress migraines and my kind teacher noticed the bruises. She realized that I was not being fed enough because I often had headaches and fainted one day. They started feeding me and called my father into the office. Then the cruelty regime became force-feeding.

He punched someone at work, and shortly after that he applied for a job in Bloemfontein. He removed me from my chance of help. Bloemfontein was hell. Tom hated the restrictive, conservative Afrikaans town. Despite being Afrikaans, he hated Afrikaner culture and forbade me to speak Afrikaans which had originally been my first language. He took out all his frustrations on me. His behaviour became more explosive and he became much more sexual.

This was partly because my mother was away a lot doing a professional training course in midwifery. I had to be the wife and warm his bed and the pre-made dinners she had left. I coped by escaping into my head. One evening he decided that I was daydreaming, and not concentrating enough on the food and might burn it.

He bashed my head into the stove and I had to have stitches on my forehead. He terrorized the poor doctor at the hospital who wanted to put in three stitches. My father insisted that I needed only one. He said that he knew best because he was a boxer and it would scar less that way. Not true. The scar is still visible. He forced me to lie to everyone and my mother about how it had happened. The only good news is that the food was not burnt.

He did these things in front of my mother too. Another time he hit me on the top of my head with a bottle, cutting my head open – and he screamed at me and swore at me for daring to cry, and be so weak, as the blood poured across my face. I still feel the pain every time a hairdresser spots the scar and asks me about it.

At the Drive-in he pushed me hard and high on a swing, and ignored me when I cried that I was going to fall. So I fell, hitting my head and was knocked out. I kept coming round and passing out in the car and was obviously seriously concussed, but he refused to get any help and threatened to hit me, if I asked, "Where am I?" again next time I came round. So I even had to remember to do what he wanted when I was concussed and passing out! The movie was *The Onion Field*. Disturbing images flashed at me every time I surfaced. My mother did nothing to help or comfort me, despite being a highly respected nursing sister - someone that her patients called an 'Angel of the Wards'.

Jasmine Rose:

It is complete bollocks that people are so different in life to their jobs. Have you noticed how so many people completely lack the skills required for their job? Or they only have those skills within that job - and it is totally absent in their home lives? The job is simply a disguise to cover the missing parts of themselves.

In the Wings

Every night I would have to say, "Nighty-night," to Tom and he would kiss me like a lover not a daughter. He would rub between my legs, in front of my mother, who turned a blind eye.

I remember her saying later on that she had noticed wetness on my clothing where he had rubbed his penis against me. (Yes, dry humping counts as molestation.) The problem is that every time she would admit something like this she would go straight into denial again, blocking it out. Or she would turn against me, saying that I was lying and had 'an over-active imagination' She would bribe or emotionally blackmail me into not telling my grandparents. I got a Barbie doll and a sewing machine that way.

At that stage there was some concern that I was going deaf and my mother took me to the doctor who said that there was nothing wrong with my hearing, but that I was in a total state of nerves, and prescribed a sedative.

Around that time my grandmother died. Or she was killed - or both. These are the circumstances, you decide:

1) Years of mental, emotional and physical abuse.

2) Near hostage-type slavery situation with a jealous, mean-spirited, revolting, alcoholic, grumpy git husband.

3) Forced to work non-stop by him at home and work.

Shortly before she died we visited them in Pretoria. Tom and Grandfather Git were rude, revolting, sneering and snide towards her. I remember her devastation and heartbreak. I could see her physically crumbling with the hurt of it all. Stabbed in the heart by the sheer mean-spiritedness of it. Technically, she died of an aneurism from all the stress, but I diagnose a broken heart. She was only in her forties. I would call it slow torturous murder stretched over decades. She stayed to be murdered out of misguided loyalty - while she quietly sang songs under her breath, about being killed softly...

But for me there was some blessing in her death. I felt that from her passing, her spirit was with me. She watched over me and protected me. I felt that she somehow calmed Tom enough in his times of rage and despair, saving me. That she guided me on how to counsel and handle him. I know that many will think that this is delusional rubbish born from my despair, but somehow I knew she was there. Desperate times can open up interesting awareness and psychic powers. There has been some considerable research done on this.

Jasmine Rose:

It does not in any way, shape or form condone abuse, making it okay though.

Lordy, I can just see some nutter online guru, or paedo totally misinterpreting that one, and making it out to be a brilliant gift!

I became a weekly border at a Catholic School at age ten. This was a solution to my problems that came to me after devouring the *Malory Towers* series. I dreamed of going to live in an orphanage or children's shelter, but boarding school was a good compromise, and I begged my mother to send me. At least it was a lot better than home and gave me respite from my father for a few days a week.

I took up piano and spent most of my practice time working out how to play the different hymns. I connected and resonated particularly with the Negro spiritual hymn:

In the Wings

'Nobody knows the trouble I've seen. Nobody knows but Jesus.'

Even though I was one of the supposedly 'privileged' white people of South Africa, I fully experienced the slave, underdog, powerless role and related to the poor African people.

The sister in charge of us was mean and bitter and she forced us to sleep without panties on 'for health reasons'. I don't know why the schools were always so obsessed with our panties. It's sick. It titillated Tom. We were forever having panty checks to make sure that we had the right pants on, or off, at the designated times. At my previous two schools, I recall having to stand to be humiliated in front of everyone in assembly for not wearing the correct horrible plasticky, crimplene-type grey-blue or sick-green bloomers. And this all happened after the bible reading and prayer in assembly. I am sure if poor misquoted Jesus had walked in he would have been enraged at children being tormented like that. I guess the teachers thought they were in danger of 'sparing the rod and spoiling the child'. Why are religious texts so violent?

Nevertheless, I was very enthusiastic about joining the school and the church. I read my bible daily and read out passages during the sermons, volunteered to clean the church and change the holy water, clean the kitchen and so on. I wanted to feel good and pious and clean. I wanted to wash away the dirt and become a nun. They were God's workers who helped stop the suffering on Earth and made it a better place.

Jasmine Rose:

But the nuns refused to help you when your mother phoned to tell them that you father was abusing you.

I will never forgive them for doing that to you, because that was when your mother crumpled, lost her resolve, turned on you and went back to him.

Their big, fat, 'I don't want to know' message assigned you to decades more of misery and danger. The Hitler nun in charge also projected your father onto you and scornfully spat that "you have the devil in you child!" projecting his evil onto you.

A worker of God surely needs to be clear on who's who in the zoo when it comes to evil?

The place that I had escaped to, became an unwelcoming place, like home. Another dictatorial regime. The spiritual home that I thought I had found was no longer safe, and I was shamed by them for something that I had not created. It was his shame, not mine!

Jasmine Rose:

Why do people support the abusers by attacking the victim? I loved the line from that play that you did choreography for. The Memory of Water *by Shelagh Stephenson. 'Always take the side of the man, no matter how crap he is!'*

Why is that? Oh yes. Because the current religious interpretations teach that men are closer to God and always right. Not a particularly logical assumption if you ask me, especially if you stop and look around!

My fear of Tom ruled supreme. Fear is not even the right word. Absolute Terror is more accurate. I remember around that time having a wart on my thumb and two on my leg, which I absolutely hated. One day my brother and I were locked in and home alone (as usual) and I decided to cut them off with a pair of scissors because the creams didn't seem to be working. The one on my leg near the hip wouldn't stop bleeding. It bled and bled and bled. I was so scared. But my main fear was Tom and what he would do to me if he found out what I had done. I was so scared that I was going to die. But I was even more scared that if I passed out and my brother was left alone, that I would be beaten up the second I came round again. I didn't know if I wanted to be healed, or I wanted to die. If I died at least he wouldn't be able to hit me. His madness confused even what would be normal prayers for survival.

Around that time Tom was fired for violent behaviour. I'm not sure of the details, but I remember my mother speaking to his boss trying to explain that his behaviour was because of some tablets that he was taking. She was his supplier of many drugs. Pain tablets, anti-depressants, uppers, downers, whatever she could get her hands on from work. He used to joke that he had only married her because of her easy access to delicious drugs. Oh, many a true word spoken in jest.

Sometimes she would steal them - or she would get a doctor to prescribe for him. It was all in the name of healing him, of course, but I wonder if those drugs weren't one of the main reasons that he stuck around. And because he had trained us to be his servant accomplices, waiting on him hand and foot.

If someone else was around, he never made himself coffee. He never even took off his own boots. I would have to be on duty the second he arrived and take his boots and socks off (yuck!), make coffee and supply him with his bottle of cold water or soda water. Heaven help me if I forgot to make sure that there was a water bottle in the fridge while he was out to be ready for his 'homecoming'. Then, most important of all, we had to gather round and listen, enthralled, as he bragged or ranted about his day.

His 'Exiting the Home' routine was even more revolting:

- A bath had to be run
- His back had to be washed
- His clothes had to be ironed in a certain way with pleats in certain places.
- His boots had to be polished and shone.
- He had to be served at least two cups of coffee.
- Food had to be packed.
- He had to be sat with while he smoked a joint and took at least four headache tablets.
- He also had to roll joint 'supplies' to smoke later at work.
- If the car was cronky it had to be pushed.

The whole departure process took at least an hour and a half out of the females of the house's schedule. Never mind if I had homework to do or a project to finish. The great lord and master was about to make a 'triumphant exit' and all had to attend him. I used to mutter, "Bloody Shah of Iran", and the words of Nancy Sinatra's 'Boot' song would go through my head.

Despite our efforts to send him perfectly turned-out for work, he was fired, and we had to move, yet again. Back to Cape Town and far away from the comforting thought

In the Wings

of relatives close by. Somehow he got a job back at the *Cape Town Theatre*. I don't know why they were so keen to re-employ a rabid racist who had a habit of decking people at work. The world works in mysterious ways, especially the theatre world. God must be baffled.

Theatre World	'Eccentricity' is accepted and praised	Good Hideout for mad people	Bad Behaviour is condoned and accepted	Management is usually made up of the most disturbed, power-hungry control freaks
Real World	People are often baffled by odd behaviour but seldom respond	People tend to judge mad behaviour, but 'not want to know' about mental health issues and fixing the problems. Too PC	Bad Behaviour is often condoned in men and seen as 'being a man' or 'being a lad'	Leadership positions are usually held by the most disturbed, power-hungry control freaks

Favourite *Facebook* status quote from William Gibson and *Urban Internet Wisdom*:

'Before you diagnose yourself with depression or poor self-esteem, first check that you are not surrounded by assholes.' (Or serving an asshole.)

jasminerose@god: Why do the willy-wagglers think that they are superior demigods to be served? Can this truly be the plan?

The story of Valentina continues:

In the Wings

INT. SCHOOL HALL - DAY

Valentina and Morag enter the dirty, dusty hall. Crumpled crisp packets and a few coins litter the floor. A shattered mobile lies rejected, thrown to the center of the hall.

Morag kicks it with a CLATTER to the side of the hall while Valentina goes to the broom closet and gets a broom to sweep the floor, carefully collecting and counting the coins.

Morag puffs on a fag as her mind wanders...

INT. STAGE - ROYAL VARIETY CONCERT - NIGHT

We see her 'dressed all posh' giving a clumsy curtsy to the Queen, while her family stand behind her and applaud, saying:

>MORAG'S FAMILY
>She's so special... she is better
>than any of us...our lives will be
>much better now...

INT. SCHOOL HALL - DAY

She comes back to earth beaming excitement -

>MORAG
>Can't wait to see their faces when
>we're on telly dancing for the
>Queen!

>VALENTINA
>We'll show them, but we need to win
>first.
>
>(BEAT)
>This needs to be about something.
>We should call ourselves Citi-Dance
>and do a citizenship message.

>MORAG
>Say what? You sound like a
>swot. What are we going to wear?
>We need to look good for royalty -
>and show these scummy slags our
>style.

>VALENTINA
>Too many dance acts have won. We
>need to make it very different.

(CONTINUED)

CONTINUED:

She raises her arms up in a V and spins, capering as she SHOUTS a competition chant:

> V - I - C , V - I - C
>
> V - I - C - T - O - R - Y!

>   MORAG
> Whatever. African Kweito is
> different enough.

MUSIC: - THUMPING, PRIMAL, SEXUAL AFRICAN STREET BEAT.

The two girls launch into the routine.

Feet stamp the beat while hair flies and shoulders shake.

Hips thrust and gyrate.

Outrageously sexual - until Valentina suddenly grinds to a halt and whispers -

>   VALENTINA
> This means nothing.

>   MORAG
> What's with you? This is what
> everyone likes.

>   VALENTINA
> We need a message.

Morag stares at her blankly.

>   VALENTINA
> About us and our lives. See my
> mobile?

>   MORAG
> Yeah - it's rubbish shite!

>   VALENTINA
> A Whitey's 'rubbish' is an
> African's treasure. My videos and
> pics of Rwanda are on here.

>   MORAG
> Well make sure that you transfere
> it. Don't let the camera crew see
> that old piece of crap.

>   VALENTINA
> Yeah sure - but we could use the
> video clips. Like Michael Jackson's
>   (MORE)

(CONTINUED)

In the Wings

CONTINUED:
                    VALENTINA (cont'd)
       'Heal the world'. We could do a
       music mix with our Keiwito and this
       song about starvation in
       Africa. Listen...

MUSIC: SWEEPING EMOTIONAL MUSIC FILLS THE HALL

                    VALENTINA
        (dancing and singing along)
       There is a woman searching food for
       her tiny girl. She prays to the
       anyone, everyone... In a life she
       didn't choose, and the pain is like
       giving birth...

Valentina is lost in another world as Morag watches her move...

INT. BRITAIN'S GOT TALENT STAGE - DAY

Valentina is in a dance dream. Music, video images on a screen behind her:

A map of Africa - with a starving woman in the foreground her hand raised in appeal, her child dying on her lap -

A map of the UK - A horn of plenty spilling out - food, clothes, technology...

She finishes, bows and speaks into the microphone saying:

                    VALENTINA
       <u>BE</u> Great Britain. You have so
       much. Interahamwe! Stand
       Together.

We see Simon Cowell in a tutu waving a magic wand... Showering her with magic sparkles that bring money for her family. She is surrounded by paparazzi, hanging on her every word.

INT. SCHOOL HALL - DAY

She comes down to earth with a realistic bump and sadly turns the volume down.

                    MORAG
       I wonder what shoes the Queen will
       be wearing? We need to get new
       ones!

                                                          CUT TO:

Chapter 5

Where are the Knights?

Afrikaans saying: *Uit oude doos*.

Translation: Out of the old box/old-fashioned

STARTING AGAIN IN SCOTLAND

Loch Lomond

'Oh, ye'll tak' the high road, and I'll tak' the low road,

And I'll be in Scotland afore ye;

But me and my true love will never meet again

On the bonnie, bonnie banks o' Loch Lomond.'

Culag Lochside Guesthouse has a spectacular view of the loch and islands.

An idyllic spot, apart from the road traffic.

The private beach sports a pier jutting out over the loch with seaplane and boats.

Feels very posh.

The floor of the pier is metal mesh so you feel like you are walking on water

You can see the lapping wavelets right under your feet.

I have a stimulating chat with the lady who serves me potato scones and eggs.

She asks what I am writing and we blether on about child and woman abuse here,

In the Wings

the extreme sexual violence statistic in South Africa, and so on.

She gets a bit worked up but is willing to talk and says:

"Someone needs to do something about it! The world needs to change."

She makes me feel like the mouse in the film *Despareaux*:

'A hero arrives when the world really needs it'.

Well – I think we need a lot of heroes.

Maybe one of the heroes is me.

Maybe us Shining Knights can change the world?

So we moved back to spectacular Cape Town and I started at a Primary School which sat nestled below imposing Devil's Peak mountain. I had the wrong uniform for ages and this was a stumbling block to making new friends (again). But I settled in well and I loved the school. It was small and friendly. What was new, was that there were boys. Lots of them. The boys outnumbered the girls 14 to 6!

We were all around eleven years old and the love interests were just starting to blossom.

Being a petite dancer with long brown hair, big eyes and long legs, I soon became the focus of some rather flattering interest. I started in the middle of the year and had a lot of catching up to do, since it was a completely different school system. The boys were wonderful. They helped me write notes and coloured in maps for me. By the end of my first term I was near the top of the class because they made it so easy for me to catch up. I had collected a large biscuit tin of love letters. My Knights in Shining Armour.

But together with attention from boys, came shame regarding my family, especially my father. Previously I hadn't been overly concerned with friends or the idea of bringing them home. I hadn't worried about needing their approval, or needing them to be approved of by my family. As soon as Tom realized that I was getting male attention he became very aggressive and made it clear that he welcomed NO boy near me or our home.

This clashed violently with the wishes of my chivalrous admirers who wanted to walk me home – and fostered the hope of being invited in. I didn't ever invite girls back either. That was partly because my father made it clear that no-one was welcome because they might see or smell his drugs, as well as the fact that I was totally ashamed of my family and how we lived. We also didn't have a telephone which made arranging visits to or from friends complicated. It is no wonder that from the age of seven I became a total bookworm and locked myself into other realities rather than dealing with the disappointment of not having friends.

Fortunately there was a ton of books that travelled everywhere with us. Some rather odd reading matter for my age. As well as the usual Jules Verne, *Asterix* and *Tintin*, I devoured J.B. Priestley, P.G. Wodehouse, D.H. Lawrence, Spike Milligan, *National Geographics* and *Mad Magazines*. My absolute favourite was C.S. Lewis and I saved up to buy the series of seven books. I lost myself in the beautiful world where there were noble thoughts and intentions. Where evil was overcome by good. Where humans, animals, nature and spirit were one. I believed that I would also be able to pass through a portal and visit such lands one day. Tom had told me that we only use about 5% of our brain power and that there was so much more that we could develop. I heard an interview with Yuri Geller and I tried to bend spoons with a stare. I jumped off tables and tried to fly. I attempted mind-talk with animals.

I read Madeleine L'Engle's *A Wrinkle in Time* science series and tried to take my consciousness deep into my own cells. Imagine if one's consciousness could visit one's own mitochondria, or go out into the furthest reaches of space? All these musings took my mind away from the treacherous disaster of my social life.

A sweet, rather overweight boy at the school called Jet was smitten with me. I gave him encouragement to raise his status with the other boys. It totally bowled him over and he made himself my champion and 'walker-home'. I allowed him to walk me only to the traffic lights because I didn't want him to know where I lived. At that time we were living temporarily in an awful pokey flat above a café on the main road. It was run-down, ugly and there was a constant roar of buses. The double-deckers thundered past giving the passengers on the upper deck a full view of us at all times of the day or night. Because of that the curtains were constantly closed which added to the dark, dingy and derelict atmosphere.

But one day Jet followed me. It was a particularly bad day because the sewerage system had exploded and there was faeces lying everywhere. I was in my slave-girl role, washing the huge pile of dishes waiting for me in the sink, when his round face appeared at the kitchen window. I felt my heart sink in my shoes and I urgently implored him to go away. Urgh, horrible!

It felt so wrong for me to be there in that setting and circumstance. I felt to the depths of my being that I was worth so much more... that this was so wrong. I felt like a diamond set into a tin ring. That might sound arrogant, but it is how I felt. I felt destined for so much better. Anyone in those circumstances SHOULD feel that. It was that conviction that kept me going, and probably prevented me from becoming a child suicide statistic. We are all worth more than that.

Fortunately we soon moved away from that flat to a nice respectable one. This was a great blessing to me and the double bonus was that it was right next to a ballet studio. It became a great place of escape. The ballet teacher soon took an interest in me and in developing my talent and offered extra free classes. I lived in tights and leotard. At first she had pegged me as being very shy and retiring and probably not able to deliver a good performance on stage. I said very little - just danced and worked away seriously at improving my technique. She would say, "Eyes up, Denise!" But I had too much to hide and my eye-line and mouth corners would drop to the floor.

In my most secret dreams I dreamt that she was my mother and that she would save me and let me live with her and her perfect family. I imagined myself in her home every day – and when I came back to reality with a bump in my own home, I felt deeply sad. But inside of myself was an inner spark of joy. Soon I would start *pointe* work. Since I was very little I had loved the shiny pink satin shoes. Fairy Princess shoes with their elegant shape and long ribbons which wrapped elegantly around your ankles - so attractive to girls. Your first *pointe* shoes are more exciting than your first kiss!

I hadn't had my first kiss from a boy yet. I was planning to wait till sixteen. I was a bit old-fashioned. Sweet sixteen never been kissed before... but there was certainly a fair bit of pressure from the boys at school to make me meet that landmark sooner! One of the older boys from the class ahead cornered me in the library and pushed me against the wall with his hand at my throat, pinning my neck to the wall. He made my frozen little self promise to hold hands with him at the back of the school hall when we watched the next Friday movie. Good news. It wasn't just my father who was scary!

Another first happened around that time. The whole class went away to school camp to learn about environment, farming and nature at a centre outside Cape Town. I was in heaven. It was bliss to be away from my family. We had all sorts of fun activities, games and competitions. There was a campfire competition which was lots of fun to prepare for. Since the boys outnumbered the girls there was only one girl per group. The boys in my group assumed that they should have the God-like position of Scriptwriter/Director even though I was better at English and a seasoned performer - and they gave me absolutely no lines. I just had to scream.

Typical, I thought to myself, I get to scream!

Jasmine Rose:

The delusional arrogance starts young! But to be fair, many film scripts were like that during that era and they were just copying... no lines for the lead ladies.

So when I did scream it was a jolly good primal scream which shook the trees and gave a few kids nightmares. Very satisfying. Despite the boys trying to keep me in the 'unimportant girl' box I was voted group leader for the last day. I was determined to show these bossy-boy-superior-shites a thing or two!

We had to trek up the mountain and cut out the invasive alien black wattle trees from Australia that were invading and killing the natural Cape fauna and flora. We were equipped with axes and saws and everyone set about cutting out the young bushes.

Throughout the camp week we had scored points daily for the best performing group for daily tasks. This was the final competition and there were 100 bean points and a big bag of sweets as prize. Everyone started chopping at the young trees that were about our height and easily manageable.

I scouted the area and found a tree about four times my height. "Let's take this one down," I said. The boys thought I was nuts, but our lovely vocational teacher Mr. D thought it a fab idea. Why the heck not? I had fallen off a horse into a cow pat and braved kissing an ostrich for the Community Newspaper photo the day before – so why not finish with chopping a tree down?

Jasmine Rose:

Didn't George Washington do that as a boy too? Maybe he just had to prove that he could do it, like you, and was proud of the achievement so was not ashamed of owning up? Honest George. I love honest leaders... like honest Abe too.

But he got shot for his individual stances didn't he? Individual thinkers like John Lennon, Jesus, Spartacus etc. all seem to have met sticky ends. Is the world ready yet NOT to switch off progressive and conscientious thinkers?

In the Wings

So we girded our loins, grabbed a chainsaw and chopped that Alien Invader down! I was like a young Lara Croft. (I love the strong actress role models like Angelina Jolie and Susan Sarandon that we have today.) The Bean Competition winners were announced in reverse order. Three other teams won the sixty beans, the eighty beans, and then finally the one hundred beans. My group was not mentioned.

We were devastated. We had definitely done more than any of the other teams! But at the last minute the Camp Leader grinned and said, "And because Denise's team went the extra mile – it gets the one hundred and TWENTY beans and the bag of sweets for extra achievement."

Oh, the joy!

Of course, I made sure that we shared the candy on the bus home with the other groups as an extra special celebration for the whole class! I love Win/Win/Win/Win when EVERYONE wins… don't you?

Shortly after arriving back home I performed in a ballet concert. I was given one of the main roles in the ballet. I was the magical Edelweiss - a healing flower in a white sparkling tutu.

My teacher gave me pep talks about needing to smile on stage and was a bit worried about me getting stage fright, but she was pleasantly surprised when I gave a sparkling, shining performance, beaming out at the audience with delight. This was the real me. The real me that could only shine out on stage, because life was too hard and painful. I needed this separate, beautiful reality where I could have moments of being me.

The gentle music, feminine themes, gorgeous costumes and the magic of the theatre cast their spell. It gave me (and my mother) moments of wonder and a glimpse of normality in our dark and difficult life.

I became one of the 'stars' of the studio. With my teacher's help I truly found self-expression and purpose and became totally dedicated. I got another taste of being a public figure when I was pictured with her in the newspaper.

She was very nurturing – but, of course, ballet is a harsh thing to do to oneself, and she was teaching me self-abuse. *Pointe* work is a form of institutionalized self-harming which was originally created to impress and titillate nobility into parting with sums of money. Apparently one of the first ballerinas, Marie Taglioni, had a father who made her practise till she fainted, to further his ambitions.

Many girls give up dancing at the *pointe* work stage. Ballet is a dedication which means very little social life and it's a crazy thing to do to your feet! But for me it was nothing worse than what I was used to. I wasn't allowed a social life anyway, and maybe the pain in my feet made the pain in my heart feel a bit less. I danced and practised until the blood poured out of my shoes.

Jasmine Rose:

And you are still struggling to get a social life. You are the Alien Upstart Colonial in a land that is famous for not dealing with personal issues. You can't ever be you, and speak your truth because people run away when you do. You are still that new girl at school with the wrong uniform. You still don't tick the right boxes. And you never will. Not fair.

The more heavenly flat next to the ballet studio was the venue for a few scenes that were so excruciatingly hellish that I will never forget them:

One day we were on the way to the library – just about to get out of my father's space, because he was in a foul mood. We often did these quick exits to the library, or nursery, or a walk around the neighbourhood to get out and away from my father's moods and violence. We were on constant high alert. This time we didn't pick up the signs and exit fast enough. I walked into my parent's room with my pile of books ready to leave and I saw Tom slapping Mary across the face. A red rage overcame me. I hurled the books with all my might across the room at his head.

Everything slowed down. I saw the books tumbling in the air in slow motion and I watched them moving towards him and thought, What have I done now?

Death was imminent. Everything moved in slow motion... my life flashed before me... and as my eyes followed the slow journey of the books towards his face, I thought, "Oh God – I'm dead." The books finally hit their target and his fury and rage turned on me.

I was grabbed, shoved, hit and dragged into the bathroom where he ripped off his thick leather belt and gave me one hell of a beating - with the buckle end. I was hit so hard that I was repeatedly sent flying around the room and onto the floor. My whole body was battered and bruised. It was a miracle that I wasn't killed or more seriously injured.

One thing that felt good was that my mother actually made some kind of protest this time and tried to get him to stop. She didn't succeed but at least she made an effort and she may have saved my life – such that it was. Afterwards I was crying in my room and she came to sit with me. Amazingly, I had the attitude of hope. I thought, well at last something so extreme has happened that must surely make her wake up and leave him. I begged her, "Leave him. He is mad. Divorce him."

She sat there on the edge of my bed and refused to hear me. Again. She said, "Yes it's terrible, yes it's wrong, but I won't leave him. I don't want my parents to know." She would rather suffer all of this and let me be beaten and abused than admit that they were right about him.

My grandmother had told her he would 'make a fool of her' and there was no way that she was going to admit it.

She said the words: "I can't admit that I was wrong and that they were right."

Those were the words that sealed the fate of her children and herself for decades of further hell.

Jasmine Rose:

Her putrid pride. This is what M. Scott Peck talks about in his book People of the Lie. *Evil is at work and hidden within communities. He says that evil is love backwards. Evol. The true evil is at work within families. Nietzsche said: "Hell is other people."*

She knew about the ongoing sexual aspect too. It was blatantly obvious. But instead of helping me, she chose to act out underhanded sabotage tactics against me out of jealousy. On the surface she appeared to be Super Mom but underneath it there was a seething anger which she took out on me in various ways.

Here is a good example:

I was dancing in an Eisteddfod and had been working very hard on three difficult solos. This was a big moment for me as the Director of the Ballet Company and Cape Town University Ballet School was judging. In the dressing room of the theatre Mary nagged on and on at me. Mary niggled, nattered and nit-picked, until I eventually lost my usual placidity and told her to stop. She gathered herself up and let rip. She shouted at me in front of everyone in the dressing room. I was so upset and out-of-body that I couldn't enjoy the dancing and went blank in the middle of the solo. I passed but didn't do particularly well.

Then she and Tom preached at me about having self-confidence. But they were smashing any shred of self-esteem every step of the way.

Jasmine Rose:

With parents like that – who needs enemies?

Huh! And I bet it was drilled into you at school and church to 'Honour your Mother and your Father'. Parents like that don't deserve any honour!

The world needs a Cinderella transformation story. At the moment so many are the servants abused by the 'ugly sisters' – or people with ugliness and harmful intent in their souls. Patriarchs feel that they have the right to 'discipline' women and children. They still say, "Women should be struck regularly". How dare they?

There needs to be a transformation where we females are recognized and seen and valued for what we are. The beauty and love we carry. As little girls all we want is to be fairies, princesses, butterflies and flowers. We carry all that beauty inside us. We bring love and nurturing.

We have the power to create and bring new souls into this world. We have magic that flows from our breasts to feed babies. That is amazing and special – yet the ugly sisters, who are born from us, resent that and want to subjugate, demean and belittle us instead – to turn us into their objects. Where did that mean-spiritedness start? When did men become stepsister bitches and enlist women to join them and do the same to each other?

Modern romances often raise these issues:

*"We women must look out for one another," Lady Danbury said to no one in particular, "since it is clear that no one else will do so." (*Romancing Mr. Bridgerton, Julia Quinn*)*

But not enough will change if the other half doesn't let it. At the moment, the meek are sitting in the ashes by the fire, dreaming of castles and princes. We need the Prince Charmings to step forward and make a stand, to help raise us to the position that we should be in, so that we can inhabit this planet in Fairness, Beauty and Love.

I wondered how much my ballet teacher heard. She lived only a few metres away. She must have surely heard the swearing, shouting, crying – and seen the bruises. She may have picked up on the signals... a typical sign of an abused child is one who tends to be quiet, look down and can't maintain eye contact.

But others can be precocious, act out or express rage.

Once, when my brother was about seven years old, I had to pull him and pinch him and drag him off a much bigger bully boy who he was strangling. The boy was turning purple and panicking but Seton was impervious. He was in such a rage he didn't know what he was doing. I had to inflict pain on him to get him to break out of the grip of fury. If I had not done that the boy may have died. Such is the suppressed rage of the child who is witness to domestic abuse.

Jasmine Rose:

Well I'm completely enraged just hearing about it! I wonder if that is why people avoid hearing about it? Is it because they are scared of their own inner rage?

Mmm. I think I need to go off and primal scream or punch a pillow now. Where are the Knights when you need them? I think I will start a Man Quest for the Modern Knight!

Tom was working at the *Cape Town Theatre* at that time and would often come home in the early hours of the morning after 'setting up' lights. I remember him going to a party where he supposedly didn't realize that there was LSD in the punch. He came home at dawn high as a kite with a palm tree that he stole from the Forestry depot. The parents made a huge song and dance about the fact that this meant that he loved my mother so much. I'm guessing that the 'make-up sex' was good.

He 'loved' her so much that he:

1) Deserted her for the night.

2) Left her to worry alone with two children.

3) Broke the law by getting drunk and high.

4) Drove to the Forestry depot and stole a tree!

What a man.

This was supposed to make up for:

1) The fact that he arrived home with the sunrise.
2) The fact that he was high.
3) Which was explained as being a good thing because, otherwise,
4) He would never have had enough strength to carry the tree.

That damn palm tree travelled with us from pillar to post through numerous moves because it was supposedly a monument to their 'great love'. Their marriage and great *Mills & Boon* romantic 'happy ending' became a horrific 16-year nightmare for me. So many children out there could tell similar Cynical Stories of Love and the horror of the old-fashioned concept of marriage.

Jasmine Rose:

I wonder how many couples out there build bad behaviour into 'macho love' and have monuments of a similar nature? Tainted Love.

denisestephani@god: What is love? Where is love?

Tom	Love & Marriage	Assumed role as Slave Master	Demoniac	Happy Ending i.e. got slaves
Mary	Love & Marriage	Slave	Got Demon Lover	Happy Ending i.e. scored point against parents
Me	Two parents united	Slave No Love	Got Demon Abuser	Totally disastrous Hell on Earth

Romeo and Juliet, Pretoria Theatre

Theatre technicians are an odd lot.

The bunch at the Pretoria Theatre *were odder than most - a law unto themselves, often high on drugs to keep awake due to the long hours. The artists had to step lively during scene changes because very little consideration was given to Health and Safety.*

One of the corps de ballet *girls got stuck with her feet on either side of a very high set of separating staircases. It was like something from an action movie scene. She was stuck between the drifting halves, legs akimbo in a semi-split. Tumterum, terum, terum Yikes! She had to fling her weight across to the one side and scramble to save herself from a five-metre drop! She did not look like an Elegant Lady in that moment...*

Denise Stephani

Another time I was doing acrobatic dance with a partner in a slippery rotating metal ring, Cirque de Soleil *style about ten metres up. They didn't think to put down any mattresses behind the set to save us if we slipped and fell. I had to insist, and got called a Diva no doubt. This was after the famous case where an actress fell into the stage lifts and nearly died.*

Jasmine Rose:

Maybe the technicians subconsciously sabotage because they are frustrated performers themselves? Quite happy to take out a few performers?

When I was in the final year of primary school, I had a weird, aggressive teacher. He was quite young and seemed to have a bit of a crush on me. He was very sadistic and used to hit the boys with a cricket bat, which I absolutely hated. But I was grateful that he gave me extra exercises in maths and encouraged my learning process ahead of the class.

Mr. D, the vocational teacher, was very interested in my 'outside the box' thought processes and would give me lateral thinking puzzles to work out. At the end of the year I got a prize for 'Consistent Attainment' That aroused some 'nudge, nudge, wink, wink, teacher's pet' comments. Tom made off-colour comments which questioned what services I might have performed to get the prize. Always smutty. They didn't know that I was working very hard to get myself out of my dire life situation.

At that time my mother pulled another one of her stunts and insisted that she thought that a tiny, perfectly normal-looking mole on my right arm was cancerous and arranged that I be operated on, a few days before my final Primary School exams. If I had the looks to enthral the boys, teachers and her damn husband, then she would make sure that it remained at JUST looks.

It was hard to study with all the fear she put into me, but I did my best as the stitches in my arm tore while I wrote my exams.

Obviously my marks would have been much better if I hadn't been dealing with the harridan-from-hell disguised as Sister Nightingale. She was so confusing. So good at her job at the hospital. Admirable. A great mother in many ways. But...

I was very excited to go to standard six at an Arts and Academics School where I could do ballet as one of my subjects. The move to the new school was good in terms of leading towards my dance career, and going to a girl's-only school was a huge relief because I wouldn't have to deal with my father's aggressive competitiveness towards the boys and male teachers.

denisestephani@god: Fathers. WTF?

denisestephani@god: Mothers. WTF?

denisestephani@god: Humans. So much potential for greatness but... WTF?

Valentina's story continues...

EXT. DAY. THE SCHOOLS GROUNDS

Valentina sits alone looking through her video clips.

                      VALENTINA
               (singing softly to herself
               more words from her FRIDAY
               song)

    I'm grateful... but sometimes there
    is too much pain."

As she sings the chorus about Friday parties, we see shots of the devastation she left behind in Africa.

Destroyed villages.

Starving people.

People with missing limbs.

Close up of Valentina looking at her missing fingers...

                      VALENTINA
        Ibuka - remember...

Contrasted with shots of well dressed UK kids throwing school laptops -

kicking over rubbish bins, breaking windows, slashing the tires of each others bikes.

Beating each other up - destroying what they have for "fun".

Then a collection of clips showing a girl at the school and her journey into sexual coercion with an older boy:

Shots of them looking at each other.

Him pulling her pony tail.

Her stealing his blazer and wearing it.

Them kissing in the school yard - her willing.

Then a shot of her resisting - not so willing.

                                                     (CONTINUED)

In the Wings

CONTINUED:

Followed by secret shots of him forcing her into the broom closet.

Then rough uncomfortable sex in the broom cupboard - her face registering shock and numbness - the door ajar, with his friends watching, sneering and laughing outside.

The bump months later.

A shot of them together. Him, angry and indifferent.

Her, ill and depressed.

A final shot of her alone, fag hanging from the mouth in front of a ugly grey counsel flat, with the pram and a dirty crying baby...

Valentina is startled by a terrible cacophony of shouting and mayhem coming O.S. from behind the gym hall. She gets up and moves quickly to towards the sound - her mobile ready in her hand.

EXT.DAY - BEHIND THE GYM HALL

Students are pushing, SHOUTING, shoving. The scene is being shot and texted. Nobody helps. As secretary Susan Gray runs in, the crowd opens up.

A 15 year boy is shaking and heaving, bloody knife in hand, as his cousin lies dying. The cousin that he's killed. Blood gushes onto the paving from a jagged abdominal wound.

Valentina examines the footage she has just shot and smiles the smile of someone who has seen far worse...then snaps the phone closed. A satisfying addition to her choreographic piece!

Chapter 6

Birthdays and Other Traumas

'Happy Birthday to you, rotten tomatoes and stew, bread and butter down the gutter, happy birthday to you'.

(Silly birthday song sung to the usual birthday tune.)

STARTING AGAIN IN SCOTLAND

Joppa, Portobello, *Rockville Hotel* 2011, Hottest September in 30 years

The sand is dotted with grateful people enjoying the unexpected Indian Summer.

White pot-bellies rise up from beach towels as the owners collapse on the sand like stranded jellyfish. Bottles of sun block are waved triumphantly at nappy-wearing toddlers, and the press stalk the beach looking for that perfect front page shot of seaside fun.

The weather is always news in the UK.

The atmosphere of festivity makes me ponder...

I have decided to try an experiment...

Every year before my birthday

which is 2nd November

(Day of the Dead and All Souls' Day),

I feel miserable and depressed and anxious.

I have pinned it down to the fact that I rue the day I was born

In the Wings

and I am not grateful to be alive.

I say that proudly and without shame.

Let those *Gratitude Journal* people come and speak to me.

How can someone who has been through the kind of thing that I have been through,

and seen the kind of things I have seen, possibly be grateful to be alive?

It's simply not logical.

Anyhoo - I am going to celebrate my birthday now, here at the beach,

a month early and see if that helps.

Might as well enjoy the good weather and have a bit of a festival right now.

Many survivors feel miserable around their birthdays.

Maybe it could be an action plan for all. A way of taking one's power back?

I will keep you posted on results.

The unfortunate thing about attending the Arts School was that my father had sexual fantasies about it. It was a girl's-only high school full of nubile, intelligent and artistic virgins. A cradle-snatching work colleague of Tom's had previously had a girlfriend in the hostel, and he had apparently climbed up the drainpipe to spend nights with her in her room. Tom was very titillated by this story. He was also very aware of my pubescent developing body.

Tom was very intent on the fact that High School meant receiving a sexual education too. He wanted to be my teacher, so he preached to me about erogenous zones, and grabbed at my sensitive, growing breasts. I cringed away from him in pain and tried to hide my breasts. I started rounding my shoulders even in ballet class and my teachers were forever nagging me about that.

I worked hard to correct all my faults. I escaped into the discipline of the class. The daily routine of *pliés*, *tendus*, *glissés* and *ronde de jambe*. They were my mantra. The safety and sanity of the regular set repetitive routine... The escape into beautiful music... Aspiring to grace...

I didn't have the best feet for ballet, but my obsession with correcting and perfecting them helped take my mind off my other problems. I stretched and bent them. I put them through pain and self-torture, which helped numb the pain in my heart.

Escape was greatly needed because in this first year of High School an event took place at home which still haunts and traumatizes me:

My father came into my room in the middle of the night while I was sleeping. He put on the light and approached my bed with rapid intent. Tom climbed on top of me and I felt him between my legs pushing against me. I cried, "NO Daddy, no!" and then everything went black. I don't know what happened next. The next morning I remembered that much very clearly, but I couldn't work out whether I had been raped or not. I don't know if there were any physical signs or not. I have a vague recollection of seeing my mother's face in the doorway. I decided that if they acted differently at all then it must have happened, but if they acted the same as usual I would know that it

In the Wings

hadn't – that it had just been a dream. Of course, he acted the same, and so did she, so I was temporarily able to assure myself that nothing had happened and that it had all been a dream.

That is obviously why I made up that test... So that I wouldn't have to face it... so that I could put myself into denial. But in the back of my mind I knew that he was a fighter, who knew dirty street tricks, like which pressure points to press to knock someone out. So I was in absolute terror for a full nine months after the event that I was pregnant. I hadn't had a period yet, so I did not have that body sign to let me know that I wasn't pregnant. Those months were an extended mental and emotional rape.

I sat in the sewing class pressing my stomach flat with my hands and praying that I wasn't pregnant. My stomach muscles were developing from all the ballet and I worried. I asked my mother if muscles changing on your stomach could mean that you are pregnant and she said yes. I was in such a state of internal agony that I found it very hard to concentrate in class and my marks dropped, particularly in maths. I didn't manage to make many friends because I was so frozen with shame and fear. Even two years later, well after that scare was over, I could hardly bring myself to look at the biology section on human reproduction. I refused to learn it. I just couldn't. It was too painful.

But it wasn't over. The molestation and threats of rape and death continued on a daily basis. Psychologically I was raped every day, and psychologically I was killed every day to keep me quiet. I was in constant terror. Yet I carried on. It's amazing what people get used to...

According to my biology class, if you put a frog in boiling water it will jump out, but if you put it in a pot of cold water and heat it slowly it will stay in the water till it starts cooking and it can no longer jump out…

I recently watched *Precious*, produced by Oprah Winfrey, and watching the film brought back all those feelings of fear. I cried for hours after - because I know that the story of Precious is the story of millions of women on this planet. I know that I am one of the lucky ones that didn't get it quite so bad. At least I didn't fall pregnant and at least I didn't get AIDS as a result of the abuse. That's something to be grateful for.

We moved to a new-build area outside of Cape Town. Even though it was far away from my school I thought that it might signal a new era. It felt more normal. My parents were investing in building a family home. It was near the beach which Tom loved. Maybe he would feel calmer and more settled? But no. It was again in an isolated area with little help available or close neighbours to hear when Tom wanted to terrorize us.

My teenage years dragged on with the continued daily abuses and ridiculous responsibilities. Apart from ballet and school I was still a prisoner locked into the house - unless it suited him to parade me at work or in front of his friends, or at my mother's work if that suited their plans.

To add to the threat he now bought a hunting knife which he wore at all times in a holder on his belt. And he had itchy feet again.

He wanted to move to a farm. I was petrified that it would mean the end of my dancing. I worried that my mother would die and I would be left totally at his mercy. It was a very realistic concern that if she were to die, that I would be permanently locked in, and the world would never see me again. He would make me his hostage wife.

In the Wings

I was grateful for the bits of freedom and social life that I was allowed as new people built and moved into the area and I made the best of it. It was mostly young families and there were no teenagers that I knew of, so I played with my brother and his friends. I became the Tomboy Ballerina of the gang. We played cricket and built tree huts and sometimes I was allowed to go and swim at the neighbour's pool. Ah, the joy to be found in brief moments of respite. Truly the stuff to write in one's Gratitude Diary…

Only I wasn't allowed one. Like all the girls in High School I started a diary and put in some pictures and thoughts. But Tom grabbed it one day, violently paging through and tearing it up in front of me. He screamed and sprayed spittle, furious at any reference to himself, or any other males that I knew. I had written nothing about his behaviour and what he was getting up to with me, but he forbade me to keep a diary. He wanted no record or witness of any description.

In his world view, I, as a female, was not even allowed to have my own thoughts.

My inner spiritual life became very important. It was the only real freedom I had. High School was Church of England influenced because it was a school sponsored by the Duke of Wellington. They made a good effort to keep it non-sectarian though, and we learnt about other global religions. The headmistress was keen on hymn singing but also went for quite modern ones, or songs that were morally inspiring, which I loved. I found the assemblies uplifting and she definitely helped steer my moral compass. I especially loved singing about 'filling the world with love'. I made that song my life anthem.

Jasmine Rose:

You still try to do the right thing and be brave and strong and true, and speak the words of love for the sake of those suffering - even when the 'Nasties' try to take advantage, or deliberately misread your motives.

'Nasties' should be your codename for the Horrible Humans who create negativity and suffering – funny how much it sounds like Nazis!

You could have a whole list of code names...

I have always thought that the name 'Muggles' for the unmagical people is code for 'Muddled-up Uglies', referring to the mean-spirited confidence killers.

Ooh – there we go. There's another one. They could also be called the 'Cofflers' because they try to kill confidence and bury it in a coffin! Ooh – I'm all excited now. I am going to make up a long list...

Somehow my spirituality got all smooshed up with my dancing. In the assemblies I would balance on the toes of one foot on a rise for the whole hymn if I could. I felt the power and energy of a universal God holding me and filling my being. I defied gravity through spiritual connection. It was a challenge being spiritual while doing something practical and earthly.

Dancers tend to be painted as being dumb tarts by society, but we have excellent brains, due to motor skills development, and more spiritual connection than most. We defy natural laws and we pray all the time to stay graceful to create beauty for others and not fall on our arses! It is a type of yoga. A moving meditation.

The travelling to school was hellish. I had to drag my unhappy brother to school and back with a stop-over at ballet. It was a nightmarish daily journey of long walk, bus, train and longer walk to get to school and then the same back again. Eventually I was allowed to join the boarding school and my brother moved to the local Junior School. It was a much better arrangement and I was extremely relieved to get out of the home for some days of the week.

Unfortunately, Tom still had his grip on me because he would give my friend Eliza and me lifts from ballet back to the hostel during the week.

Often it was just me that he gave a lift to. Then he would take me on 'dates' to the *Steak Ranch* and behave inappropriately. He would speculate as to whether people thought he was my boyfriend. I was a puppet in his kinky fantasies. He would also stop the car in the dark, spooky park, smoke a joint and grope me. While he was driving he would force me to put a hand onto his leg and then he would push it up higher and higher till it was touching his crotch. I couldn't remove it, or he would lash out in anger.

He did many inappropriate things. He sent me a bouquet of flowers to the hostel on Valentine's Day accompanied by a revolting lecherous card with a mouth and licking tongue on it. It said 'You're Delicious' I was devastated, angry and humiliated – not to mention scared. At this stage he kept shoving his head in my crotch, and informing me that he was dying to perform oral sex on me. I lied to Eliza about who the card was from. I made up a boy admirer. The joys of being in the grips of a dangerous liar who forces you to lie to all the people you are close to and care about...

Thank goodness for Eliza. I had a few good friends by then, but she was my Very Best Friend at the hostel and of my life. We have stayed in touch over all the decades. We did fun boarding school things. Picnics on top of the cupboards, midnight feasts in the bathroom and a few fabulous practical jokes. We took great delight in putting salt in the sugar for the tea of the headmistress and watched in admiration as she refused to respond and actually drank the tea! We created a 'ghost' from a white pillow case on a broom and two prunes for eyes and frightened a group of girls into a screaming frenzy when we poked it outside their window in the middle of their midnight feast. We shared romance novels and crushes. She taught me how to shave my legs and use a tampon.

My mother had opted out of these lessons and forbade me to do either, causing me embarrassment and difficulty at ballet. A minor rebellion, but sweet nonetheless…

I had read all the Enid Blyton *Malory Towers* books, and I have to say that the hostel compared quite favourably. We got bored of the same old food though, so we made up inventions like Apple and *Marmite*, or Fish Paste and Sugar sandwiches.

Eliza danced, but was also a budding actress. I was so impressed with her when at age fourteen she did Salieri's monologue from the movie *Amadeus* for a drama competition. A young girl taking on an old man's role. She went on to do very well as an actress.

I loved theatre and also performed in the School Play, *Little Women*. I danced as a doll come to life in the dream scene. There was great excitement because we had a couple of guest boys from the Boys High performing too. But surprise, surprise - they created drama.

One of them got into an ego trauma and threw his toys, storming out of the rehearsal, slamming the door as he went. We all looked on in horror, mouths hanging open at the unusual display of temper and bad behaviour. We were not used to this in a girl's-only school.

The lovely rotund teacher took us off for a milk shake and explained:

"Girls this is what you need to know about men: Whether they are six or sixty, they are still only six."

I never forgot that. The young man was acting out in a sociopathic way because he knew that it would make him seem exciting and get him attention from the girls. He was very successful at this and had a whole fan club following. He was simply welcomed back into the fold and made a fuss over when he came back to the next rehearsal. A young, budding Tom-type...

This must be sooo frustrating for the Good Guys out there. Why have girls been brainwashed to like the sociopathic 'Bad Boy'? And why do parents indulgently say: "Ah well, boys will be boys," when the same behaviour would invoke absolute horror if done by a daughter? And it goes on into adulthood. Things that a woman would be shunned for is seen as simply, 'A guy being a guy'. Harmful double standards.

Pretoria Theatre, Le Rendezvous

Le Rendezvous is a frothy ballet about love and a touch of intrigue. It is about couples meeting up and love blooming in a fashionable park. We wore delicate white debutante dresses with bows, sashes and matching hats. We felt très élégante. *There were little comedic moments in the piece, and the audience was transported through the various foibles and fancies of love relationships.*

We were just finishing off the last finale section where the couples meet up and leave the park together, love matches concluded. The Ladies and Gents enter from separate sides of the stage then join up in the centre. I had to do a soutenous *twirl and then fall forward into my partner's arms with mine around his neck - and he was to exit stage centre rear by sweeping me along, running backward to exit gracefully through the park gates. Unfortunately on this occasion he tripped over his own feet and fell over backwards, pulling me forwards to fall on top of him. My skirts flipped over my head, and I was tipped, tail up, with legs flailing at the audience!*

As I picked myself up I thought up a quick acting save. I stomped one foot and thrust my hands on my hips, showing my crossness, and minced off. Leaving my partner to shrug at the audience and run after me as if it was part of the story. We heard an appreciative giggle from the audience and a smattering of applause. I was rather proud of our ability as young dancers to have an accident, but pull it off and make it look like it might have been part of the story.

The management didn't concur and gave us a roasting in front of the whole company – but I think that they were secretly impressed with our survival tactics...

A pity they couldn't just admit it, and praise us instead of acting like Muggle Coffler Nasties!

In the Wings

Early one Saturday morning we were on our way to the Ballet School. It was a few weeks before my Royal Academy of Dancing Intermediate exam, so extra practice was very important.

Later in the day we were to go away for the weekend to some hot water springs. It was pouring with rain and cold, but there was an air of excitement. As we drove along I enjoyed the view of the dramatic Table Mountain and Devil's Peak in the mists.

My father, as usual, was high on his morning pre-departure joint and ticking over nicely.

We were driving along the highway in the usual way. Faster than everyone else, and overtaking all the slow 'idiots' on the road. I didn't feel too anxious because Tom was in a better mood than usual, and there wasn't as much anger in his driving. So when the car started veering all over the road I thought that he was doing one of his little scaring jokes that he was inclined to do from time to time. He would also drive off without us, leaving us to run after the car. My thoughts were more, Oh grow up! rather than Oh, my God we're going to have an accident!

Next thing the world was swirling as we went up the embankment and headed for a pole. Everything faded into blackness. I must have broken the window with the back of my head, and my brother and I were thrown right out of the car. The car rolled, hit the embankment again and tipped back over onto its wheels, neatly parking itself alongside the road. This was very lucky as the cars behind would otherwise have been involved, especially given the poor visibility and rain. I was told all these details later, since I was knocked out cold before I even hit the ground. I fortunately landed in the gutter and not the middle of the road and my brother landed on his feet and continued running up the embankment.

My father freaked when he saw me lying in the gutter. He ran to me and tried to pick me up which is a stupid thing to do. If I had injured some vertebrae that could have been the end of me. My mother tried to tell him this, but as usual he ignored her, even in her field of expertise.

My arm and neck were cut and red with blood. Fortunately, someone stopped and took my mother, brother and me to the famous Groote Schuur Hospital. This is the hospital where Christian Barnard performed the first famous heart surgeries with baboon hearts. I remember lying across the back seat with my brother comforting me, telling me we were going to a good hospital. He was so sweet and brave and every time I came round he would tell me that I was going to be okay. When we got to the hospital and they started cleaning up the cuts on my arm, then the poor courageous young thing tossed out his breakfast and practically passed out himself.

So I had the usual, X-rays, bandage on arm, a soft collar round my neck which was whip-lashed and cut. My arm was roughly cleaned by a brusque nurse who used water that was way too hot and burnt me. She wouldn't believe me when I said it was too hot. To her it was fine because she was warm inside the building, but I had been out in the cold and the rain so I was freezing, and the contrast meant that the water felt boiling to me.

The reason why I am going into such detail about this, is because it is such a good example of how insensitive people are to your pain and how quick they are to say, "Oh rubbish, I'm not feeling what you're feeling. I don't relate, so your reality can't be." Even with the purely physical. So even more so with the unseen emotional issues...

Jasmine Rose:

Ooh, that type of person deserves a name too. Let's see – someone who displays a refusal to listen, therefore causing pain: A Reflistopain. Ha, my new vocab is growing!

It was decided that we would still go on the spa holiday which was booked and paid for. The parents decided that it would be a good way to relax my torn muscles and clean out my wounds in the natural mineral water. I was grateful for this consideration. It gave me hope that there would be a change and that Tom would treat me better. If I had died he would have been jailed for manslaughter since he was driving without a licence – so there was something to celebrate!

But the next day we were sitting as a family in the bubbling water in one of the large, enclosed private jacuzzis, when my father, with a revolting smirk on his face, stretched his foot across the pool. He thrust it between my legs and pushed the material of my bikini bottom aside to stick his big toe up my vagina. This is a rape I remember clearly. He glowered at me and the threat in his eyes was clear. "React, and show to your mother and brother what is happening at your peril!"

It was physical, mental, emotional and spiritual rape. I was already in shock from the accident and recovering from trauma, but he chose to add to that, sending me completely out-of-body and out-of-mind from the sheer horror of his actions. I wore the mask, but I was especially devastated because he had been carrying on about how upset he had been when he thought I might die, giving me hope for more appreciation and respect. A wake-up call? But no.

Jasmine Rose:

Mmmm. But I suppose that the self-helpers would tell you that you should be grateful that you were just goosed and not buggered!

Lordy, your vagina would have something worthwhile to say in the Vagina Monologues...

Things were getting worse. Tom made me look at porn. He said that he wanted to get me onto contraceptives and educate me about sex. He said better to learn from him, 'The Expert', than from boys who didn't know what they were doing.

If I even accidentally looked at a member of the opposite sex when we were out he would hit me and call me a whore.

I tried again to get my mother to acknowledge what was going on and to do something about it, but she just grabbed me by the shoulders and glared into my face saying:

"Look – I don't want to know". I ran to my room and hid, writhing in agony, hugging myself and rocking as the words of a song that I learnt in a modern dance solo went round and round in my head - words about a puppet on strings waiting for love.

Jasmine Rose:

Bless you my poppet, you really need to be heard.

But do you think that people will believe your story, or do you think that they will say that you are making it up? I'm not sure why any daughter would ever WANT to make something like that up about her own father or mother. Most children just want a normal, happy childhood. Even if you were making it up, it would mean that something must have been very wrong in your childhood to make you want to do that.

I know you, and I know you are telling the truth for a greater good. It is a humanitarian issue that affects the whole world. You are a small part of a world story, and want to make a difference. You want to hold up the mirror, but much of the world doesn't like looking in the mirror.

If they don't like what they see they want to smash it - and the holder-upperer.

Luckily there are many witnesses to his general public craziness... but do the witnesses have courage to stand as witness?

Trying to make sense of it with a table:

Me	Desperate, fearful situation	Crying for help
Mother	Allowing situation to continue	"I don't want to know"

I love Queen. *Bohemian Rhapsody* nearly finishes me off... Maamaaa, ooo ooooh!

Fat Bottomed Girls reminds me about my mother and her complexes. She hated her nose and hated her bottom. It is ridiculous that she spent so much time in front of mirrors obsessing about that, when she could have been dealing with the nightmare of what was happening in our lives. She was suffering from the same Nero Complex which seems fashionable, 'Fiddling while Rome is burning'.

And yet, like most children, I loved her unconditionally. I thought she was perfect. I thought that she was where the sun shone best.

I put up with it all in silence out of love for her…

Cape Town Ballet, Orpheus in the Underworld

Whilst we are on the bottom theme I will tell you about how I met the man at the top. By flashing my bottom!

Cape Town Ballet does a very fun and entertaining version of Orpheus in the Underworld, *or* Orifice in his Underpants *as the witty techies used to call it.*

They came up with smutty alternative names for most things…

Air on the G-string *became* Wind in your Jockstrap.

Cinderella *was* Cinder-fella.

Sleeping Beauty *was* Bleeping Sooty *and so on.*

I guess when you have to watch and listen to a show so many times you have to find ways of entertaining yourself. But I digress…

In the Third Act, in the Underworld scene, there was devilish entertainment in the form of saucy French cancan dancers. Ooh la la! I was one of them. I loved the fishnets and the high kicking. I was a little dubious about flashing the knickers, but of course the audience loved it. Young, old, rich or poor. It was all quite tricky to do in pointe *shoes, but I revelled in the challenge and threw myself with joy into the cartwheel and splits at the end.*

We performed the ballet for a fundraiser Gala Event. There was a big cheese and wine do after with all the rich, famous and influential. I was delighted to shake hands with President FW de Klerk and his wife. Shortly after that he was to win the Nobel Peace Prize, together with Mandela, for their work in transforming South Africa. I cared deeply about my country and was pleased with the changes, so was very honoured to meet him.

But it felt a bit odd and surreal. Cancan, flash-me-pants and then, "Oh-how-do-you-do sir?" That's cultural dance diplomacy!

Jasmine Rose:

I have to get to the bottom of this. I have to get it off my chest. Most of your stories seem to involve bottoms. What IS all this obsession with private body parts and behinds in the human race? It keeps rearing its ugly head. We are forever making boobs whilst obsessing about bums. Like some famous politicians whose names we won't mention...

The next blow in life came when my father decided to stop my dancing – the only joy in my life.

He took me away from my much loved, supportive and kind ballet teacher. She was mentoring me and believed in my talent and he took me away from her. She wanted me to enter prestigious competitions in Britain and Europe. The Adeline Genée and the Prix de Lausanne.

She was hoping to get me a scholarship to study at the London Ballet School. I think that she sensed something of my plight and wanted to help me to get a new start in life using my dancing talents.

He took me away from her because she was giving me love, help and support. This is what he always did. Obviously he was scared that they knew what he was up to, and so we moved or he removed me when anybody got close, but I also think he simply didn't want me to get caring and support from anybody. He wanted me to be totally isolated and dependent on him and his tainted love. He used my dancing for manipulation and to make me collude and keep silent about my abuse. It was the only thing in life that gave me some joy and freedom but it was also used to shackle me and keep me silent in the family situation. And now he was upping the power game by removing it for a while.

I was tempted then to spill the beans, but I knew that if I did manage to get help and went to a shelter (which was my secret dream) that I would not have the opportunity to continue with my ballet lessons. Somehow I didn't think that I would be adopted by nice people who would give me that. I guess I felt too worthless and soiled. The chance of being adopted had already been there when I was born, but been denied me. I assumed that the same thing would happen again. So I was caught in a dark vacuum without dance…

Tweet to God: Why all the manipulation and violence hidden by deafening silence?

The story continues…

In the Wings

```
INT. BOTANICAL GARDENS - GLASSHOUSE - DAY
                    VALENTINA
          This is how I imagine the world
          should be.  It reminds me of the
          few beautiful, peaceful places in
          Africa.

                    MORAG
          God!  Look at this plant.  It looks
          like a whole bunch of stiff
          willies.

She looks at the sign.
          It's called a Wandering
          Screwpine.  Makes sense.

                    VALENTINA
          I love the creepers going up to the
          top. They aspire to higher.  This
          is my favourite place.  There's a
          little robin that talks to me.

                    MORAG
          Crazy chick!  You need a
          boyfriend.  Stop hanging out with
          birds and worrying about the world!

A family of parents and young children enter with their
hand-held listening guides.

                    FATHER
          Come on - let's listen to the story
          of the Screwpine.

                    MORAG
               (snickers a dirty laugh and
                whispers aside)
          They're a bit young for sex-ed Dad.

She looks at the sign next to her:
          Cycad Sex - setting the seed...
               (putting on a TV Ad voice)
          who needs porno to get you
          hot?  Just visit the Botanics!


                                             (CONTINUED)
```

CONTINUED:

INT. BOTANICS MAIN GALLERY - DAY

Valentina has placed a small sound system on a bench - the MUSIC IS PUMPING and they are lost in their world of dance, inspired by the setting - leaping, turning, jumping, dropping, flying.

INT. LEISURE CENTRE DANCE STUDIO - DAY

Valentina enters. Morag is waiting for her, dragging on a sneaky fag, looking guilty.

Valentina rushes to put on her music. A great remix of her two songs!

As she starts showing her new moves, the door bursts open and Morag's MOTHER storms in f-ing and blinding under her breath. The school secretary Susan Gray is with her.

> MOTHER
> Skipped school again! They can take you away. You're rubbish! I've had it.

She grabs Morag by the arm and drags her out, totally ignoring Valentina.

> VALENTINA
> I can't do it on my own...

Susan shrugs sympathetically and leaves.

EXT.DAY - PAVEMENT OUTSIDE A TRAIN STATION

Valentina is moving down the dank, dirty pavement towards the station, stamping her feet and creating a rhythm. muttering her own rap poem under her breath...

> VALENTINA
> Fugly, Fugly - this world is fuckin' ugly. Social services got my friend. Beginning Ah - aah? Or the end? Flying hope around the bend?

She looks around at her environment and pulls a face. As she stamps up to the ticket window she shouts:

> VALENTINA
> Fugly, fugly, it's all fuckin' ugly!

The grumpy-git face of the ticket officer is a picture of disapproval as he tuts and harrumphs.

(CONTINUED)

In the Wings

CONTINUED:

                    GRUMPY GIT
     What's your name? I should report
     you.

                    VALENTINA
     Valentina. That's V for Valentina.

She holds up two fingers in a V and then twists her
hand around to give him the 'Fuck You' sign.

EXT.DAY - STATION PLATFORM

Valentina sits on a bench waiting.

EXT. MAGIC LAND - DAY

She mentally transforms the station. A world with brightly
painted buildings, lawn and trees. Flowers everywhere - no
dirt - happy people. She is dressed brightly and is wearing
a t-shirt that says:

'Yes to Colours. No to Grey Grumpy Gits!'

Behind her is a Botanics poster that says:

No Biodiversity No breakfast

Chapter 7

High School Ends

Afrikaans saying: *Stille water, diepe grond, onder draai die duiwel rond.*

Translation: Still waters, deep ground, beneath the devil swirls around.

STARTING AGAIN IN SCOTLAND

Joppa, Portobello, 2011

I am in my Rockville lighthouse room looking out at the far wide sea. It is high tide, but a gentle high, with lapping at the edges. No waves today. Calm and gentle. Trickling over the ancient rocks. That is how I feel sometimes... Ancient. I know too much and have seen too much. Too much of the dark side.

It is good for me – these visits to Portobello, to feel the comfort of the sea and nature. The weather has been kind. There has been a lot of light. It feeds my soul and soothes my troubled mind. There is a more positive energy and way of life in this part of Scotland.

I gaze across the waters of the Forth and the morning sun shines on the shipping buildings creating a glittering golden light which bounces off them brightly turning them into beacons of light and hope.

If industrial buildings can be transformed by light into citadels of golden splendour, can I perform alchemy and transform all the darkness I have seen in my life into something that can bring shining hope to other survivors and to the world?

I need the Midas Touch.

About six excruciating months later, when I was fifteen, Tom allowed me to go back to afternoon ballet class but with another teacher at the University of Cape Town Ballet School which was bigger, and where I was less likely to get one-on-one attention. It was such a relief to be back in full training. I had been practising by myself at home and school, but it wasn't good enough, and I could see that the other girls in the ballet class at school were overtaking me. I auditioned and was accepted into the *Youth Ballet Company*. This was quite an honour because usually it was only for university students, eighteen plus. But child prodigies were very popular in the ballet world of Cape Town at the time. There were three of us still in high school who had already pushed ourselves to a student standard by that early age. The old South Africa was very influenced by Russia and we had to be superhuman. It was the time of Golden Girl and Zola Budd, and we took the superhuman aspirations seriously. It was a strange clash in society. The true African people were being made to feel inferior and remain less than what they were, but white people were expected to show their Aryan Race superiority. That was a huge pressure and injustice on both sides of the coin. White South Africans were pressured to achieve despite boycotts and being cut off from the world. We were expected to show the world that we could be better than them despite the sanctions. Massive stress for kids!

As the regime started changing, one of Balanchine's exballerinas came out from New York and we learnt *Waltz Fantasy* and *Valse Fantasia* which we performed in various venues. People came from the Royal Ballet and taught us the Fairy Solos from *Sleeping Beauty*. I was the Fairy of the Crystal Fountain and we wore the professional Ballet Company tutus. It made me feel special and sparkly and new.

In my final school year we went on a tour to Port Elizabeth, but my father was so obsessed, that he wouldn't let me go alone. He insisted that he should come along as the driver and lighting technician. Except that being the rebel outlaw that he was, he had no damn driver's licence. My poor ballet teacher was dominated into agreeing to all this, but found out at the last minute that he had no driver's licence and had to bring along her husband's business driver instead at a huge extra cost. I felt absolutely terrible. She was clearly pissed off, and considering that she had sponsored me for summer schools and classes it was a big insult, and a disgusting Tom con-job. I don't think that the other girls liked having him along either, although some of them may have thought that he was different and 'cool'. I stayed with a ballet teacher in PE, thankfully, and not with my father in the hotel. What a blessing that was, though he insisted that I visit him there and have lunch with him. I was terrified that he was going to rape me there.

How did I feel during that tour? Frozen with terror. I think I must have been even more quiet than usual. Tom had caused enough drama – I just wanted to be invisible.

But I kept up the act as usual. I acted my innocence and naïvety. The performance was so Oscar-winning that the girls thought that I was too ladylike, prissy and pure to be told of much that they were up to. They were up to the party, drug and sex antics, but very few told me anything because they had the impression that I was totally dedicated to study and dance and knew nothing of the

In the Wings

world. My father was the 'King of Sex, Drugs and Rock 'n' Roll', but they thought that I knew nothing. Huh! I would complain, and want to know, but they would giggle and keep quiet. One friend bought me a little round badge that said:

'I think I must be a mushroom because everyone feeds me shit and keeps me in the dark.'

My nickname became Denny-mushroom after the South African button mushroom brand. I don't know what it is with me and mushrooms. They always seem to crop up. My father used to say that I had a 'button-mushroom nose' when I was little. Although he was probably being a game-playing bitch because he knew that my mother had a complex about her Roman nose...

I don't mind being a button mushroom. Mushrooms grow from earth, manure and darkness, but they rise up and become beautifully formed, light and versatile, and they serve nature by giving nutrition to all. They make the world a better place.

I absolutely flourished at boarding school, especially now that I had my dancing back. My marks went up to As. Around me people were homesick and angry about being sent to boarding school. There was attention-seeking bulimia, suicidal attempts, sneaking out etc. but I was in bliss. To be fair I had the advantage of being able to go out to ballet two afternoons a week which certainly helped, but I would have been very happy to be a termly boarder. I hated being picked up on Fridays and I hated that my father mostly insisted on dropping me off on Monday mornings instead of Sunday nights like he was supposed to, and that he slobbered all over me in front of the school. It was so revolting it practically curdles my soul just thinking about it. He was usually high and stinking of weed from the joint that he had just smoked. It was sick, sick, sick! My whole aura felt grey and old and brown at the thought of it. At least once I got there I was safe and I could have a more normal life.

I worked incredibly hard. I wanted to show my parents that it was good to have me there because my reports were so good. I got two A+ grades for History and Biology Projects and a special mention from the Headmistress. My Biology project was chosen for a competition. I was working my butt off to keep myself in a safe space. But as usual the bliss didn't last...

They took me out of the boarding school because they sold our house and bought a farm up north near the Kruger National Park. We moved to a rented flat again. This was close to the railway and easy access to school and ballet, so they said that I had to be at home. I was to be the do-it-all slave again, with little time to study. When I was trying to study Tom loved ordering me to do things, or he would come up behind me for a grope and try to stick his tongue in my ear to distract me. He was totally invasive. My parent's quietly delighted in the dropping of my marks and the fact that I would not be able to take up the boarding school Prefect position to which I had been appointed...

Jasmine Rose:

Fuckin' bitches! You had the opposite experience of the cliché. Parents who DIDN'T want you to do well at school! A real life variation on the Cinderella and her ugly sisters theme!

Or like Sleeping Beauty with the Evil Fairy and its sidekick casting a spell and making life impossible for the poor heroine so that she is sent into a half-dead state of sleep.

SWEET SIXTEEN, NEVER BEEN...

Things went from bad to worse because now I was at the legal age of sexual consent. My father became totally fanatical about that fact, and extremely possessive and jealous. He went through a phase where he was trying to get me to take the pill and hard drugs like LSD and marijuana – no doubt so that I would be more vulnerable and available to him. But I refused. Another battle to fight. I often think that I have had the equivalent of SS training. Between the psycho and the ballet discipline and pain, I have had to become stronger than most humans on this Earth. Always living beyond the breaking point. Constant fight, challenge and discipline. Every day I would have to kick, hit, scratch, bite to keep him off me. I had to talk him down. Decades of boot camp. But the main fight was simply to remain me, and not be hardened and changed by it all.

I became asexual. Disassociated with sex and anything to do with it. Alienated from life and the darkness...

Jasmine Rose:

Huh! The prick put you into a deep, near-dead sleep...

And yet – I felt sorry for him. I was his counsellor too. He would cry out his pain and worries. They were probably crocodile tears a lot of the time, but he was in mental agony. He would say:

"You would all be better off if I was dead." He was right. But I comforted him. Us females are trained to forgive too much.

So the High School Finals happened. My marks had dropped horribly. I still did well in Ballet and okay in the academic subjects, but I was so out-of-body that I couldn't co-ordinate my fingers in my typing exam, so nearly failed. I scraped through. I would have panic attacks during the speed tests, my fingers would go all over the place and I would make millions of mistakes. Post-Traumatic Stress Disorder at work…

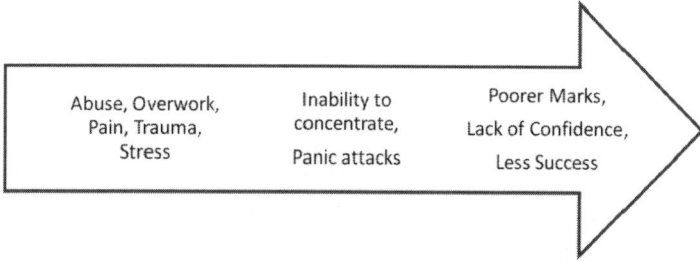

Abuse, Overwork, Pain, Trauma, Stress → Inability to concentrate, Panic attacks → Poorer Marks, Lack of Confidence, Less Success

Just before the school exams I had auditioned for Cape Town Ballet. My main competitor got in but I didn't. It was a huge blow. I was dealing with too much. Being saved by being taken into the ballet company had been my dream and it was smashed. They held a second audition a few weeks later but I didn't go, I couldn't face being smashed a second time in the space of a few weeks. I feared I might go mad like Giselle. My ballet teacher told me off for not going, because she felt that the company Director would have chosen me at the second audition. It would have helped if she had encouraged me to go to the second audition, but she didn't. She didn't speak to me much. She was still angry with Tom and couldn't understand my inability to communicate easily with her like the other girls did. She may have thought that my silence was ingratitude and lack of ambition.

My family were moving up to Pretoria to be closer to the farm. There was some talk of me staying in Cape Town and going to the University Ballet Course but I knew that they couldn't afford it and that it would mean massive student loans etc. Tom would never have allowed it anyhow. There was no chance that he would leave me alone and unguarded in Cape Town. He was my prison guard and keeper. There was no way that he would tolerate leaving me alone. His death/suicide threats escalated. I was trapped.

I comforted myself with the thought that the Pretoria Ballet was in a much better situation. There was so much drama and scandal going on at the Cape Town Company at that time, and in many ways I was keen to break out of the box that I had been placed into of being technically strong and a good performer, but shy, silent and lacking in confidence in the rehearsal process. And, of course, I wanted to escape the reputation of being the daughter of the maniac father who constantly caused trouble. At least in Pretoria people didn't know us. It might be a fresh start...

Later my mother blamed me for not choosing to stay in Cape Town. She said that if things were so bad with him I could have made that choice. That was just her denying responsibility.

Jasmine Rose:

All this happy-clappy New Age spouting of, "There's always choice", is complete rubbish. Ask a mother of starving children in Somalia. The only choice a mother has is to watch her child starve to death, or smother it towards the end so that it doesn't suffer too long. Fab choice. Utter Bollocks. Therapists hearing your full story have agreed that your only real choice was whether to commit suicide or not – and suicide was the more logical choice! So often there is no choice – especially for women and children caught up in the machinations of men. The movie Thelma and Louise *demonstrates this point perfectly.*

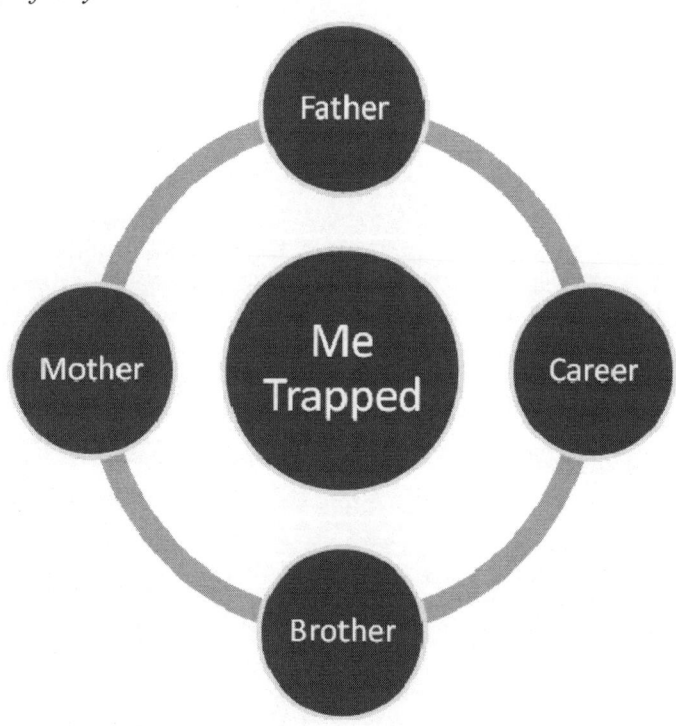

In the Wings

But the one thing I had was that I could dance. Dance in the studio, and dance through life – bobbing and weaving and wending my way through the treacherous labyrinth…

Jasmine Rose:

I believe that you recently studied Dance Movement Psychotherapy…

Don't you think that a lot of the dance therapy claptrap that has been created makes something simple and healing and fundamental to life, more Pretentious for the pompous pontificating techno-world?

Dance because it's good for you and part of the natural design of the human being!

The same could be said for singing and music. Art and storytelling are also fairly fundamental to being a human being. It is simple – like breathing, sleeping, eating, mating. It is part of who we are as a species. Why has there been this great separation – this great rift created? Why did it become 'posh' for the upper classes, 'arts' for the arty-farties, or 'feminine' for females?

When did Dance lose its value and its place? When did it become 'Just your body, not your brains'?

Oh yes, that's right: When men realized that women are generally better at it, and decided that that fact minimizes the Male God-like status! And WHY can't men see beyond the bendy sex potentials? All they see is ankles around ears.

Dancing is a soul thing, an expression of the Divine. Women dance for women and the universe, but men think that it is all about them… about offering sex on a platter.

They disrespect us for dancing, when to us it is prayer…

Denise Stephani

'The Scarlet Whore, indeed they snarl at, but like right well a (DANCING) whore in scarlet.' Alan Ramsay (1686 – 1758). Epistle to Mr H.S. at London.

The story continues…

In the Wings

INT. TRAIN CARRIAGE - DAY

The carriage is full - but there is one seat left.

JOHN MC GARVEY, a podgy, grey suited accountant is taking up two seats. His briefcase and paperwork are covering his lap and spilling about him.

John is oblivious - frantically jotting down numbers. He is shaking and twitching.

A fat old lady across the aisle notices Valentina being roughly rocked by the carriage movement and leans across:

                    FAT OLD LADY
   Shove over!

John blushes and reluctantly gathers everything onto his lap, letting Valentina squeeze through to the window.

EXT. PASSING VIEW - DAY

Valentina looks out of the window and her super-colouring animation mind kicks in again. She recreates the dull dirty buildings passing outside with brightly painted colours and lights.

INT. TRAIN CARRIAGE - DAY

Nexto her John stares blankly forward, lost in his dream...

INT. BRITAIN'S GOT TALENT STAGE - NIGHT

John is in a stylish black suit looking 10 pounds lighter tap dancing away with brilliance - playing banjo honky-tonk blues at the same time. A double act! And the CROWD GOES WILD. SIMON, PIERCE and AMANDA jump to their feet in awe. A standing OVATION!

INT. TRAIN CARRIAGE - DAY

John doesn't notice that the train has pulled up to his stop. He breaks out of his dream as people stream out the carriage. He tries to gather his things from the top shelf but his laptop CRASHES onto the floor, followed by his bag - spilling it's contents - including his tap shoes.

                                                (CONTINUED)

CONTINUED:

                    JOHN
          Jesus! The firing squad...

Valentina helps him. He rushes towards the closing door.

At that moment Valentina looks out of the window and sees the dowdy school secretary, Susan Gray, slipping and falling on the icy platform outside. Her ankle looks broken and she is in shock as a crowd gathers.

We witness her near-death flash sequence:

Susan as a shy browbeaten secretary -

The headmaster shouting and sneering at her -

Throwing paperwork back in her face...

Then flashes of her secret persona:

DELILAH DEVINE - a teasing, emasculating Sex Goddess.

At Britain's Got Talent -

Dancing in only a g-string with two large ruby red feather fans to conceal and reveal -

The faces of Simon and Pierce -

their goggle-eyed stares -

Enormous Erections in the trouser dept...

Susan comes to reality. She is flat on her back, legs in the air... with a broken ankle.

Behind her a glimpse of poor John, pulling at the door, stuck. His face says "I am going to get fired" as he smashes his tap shoes against the window in frustration.

In the train window we see Valentina giggling.

Chapter 8

College Collage

Afrikaans saying: *Knyp die kat in die donker*.

Translation: Pinch the cat in the dark. (hidden activities)

STARTING AGAIN IN SCOTLAND

Edinburgh Festival

Living in Edinburgh is like living in a ballet set. The magnificent sandstone buildings and Castle lit up across the skyline at night. As a little girl I used to gaze in wonder at the painted backdrops of the ballets like *Giselle* or *Sleeping Beauty* thinking such beautiful settings were only possible in fairy tales.

But no – Edinburgh has them!

Millions of people flock to the city every year to enjoy the magical splendour, bobbing and weaving through the streets like a bunch of goblins and gremlins, rushing to venues and whichever festival event happens to be on their itinerary. This is Festival City. An endless stream of Film, Creativity and Book festivals –

and, of course, the famous Edinburgh Arts Festival...

(The Mad Parliament Buildings, crazy road systems and parking nightmare are famous too. As are the big, beefy, intimidating traffic warden mafia, who patrol and aggressively slap a ticket on for the most minor transgressions - and that's just the women!

It's a very functional, deliberately dysfunctional system, which makes a fortune for the privatized parking company and council. Don't even get me started on the metaphor of the Tram Disaster… It is not a coincidence that the word 'Muggle' was coined in Edinburgh.)

Aah, but one forgets all that when one is in the tranquillity of the glorious Princes Street Gardens, or even better – The Botanics! There are few cities that can boast of such a peaceful setting within a city as the Water of Leith Walk, with its Temple to Hygeia, the Goddess of Healing, and Modern Art Gallery en route.

This is a strange city with fickle, changeable weather and citizens. There are rowdy drunks with a high hidden violence factor, but it is a haven to many. The climate creates dour depression and coldness of heart, but not a bad place for my boys to grow up after surviving the far worse troubles of Africa…

- - -

I seemed to be bouncing around the country my whole life through. We were back up in the Transvaal. Pretoria Dance College was a relief when it started. My grandparents paid for my first term and I was grateful for that, but I was stuck in a small flat with my mad family again. Being near his family seemed to make Tom become even more cracked than usual.

But I made some friends at the College. Helen and I connected very quickly. We were the two goody-goody-hard-working girls. We didn't party and we took our study and dance very seriously. What worked well for me was that I was clearly at a much higher level than the others of that year, and I was at the top of all my classes, including the academic subjects like anatomy, kinesiology, choreology, music theory etc. It was so wonderful not to be pushed down to second or third place due to favouritism and family connections. It was so good to feel like I wasn't the charity case who was lucky to be there at all.

There are stories of how scholarship and bursary kids get treated well and encouraged, going on to great heights, with people helping them overcome the obstacles of their background. And 'reality' programmes often give a completely false impression. I can tell you from experience – it ain't so lovely in the real world. People want to keep you in your box so that they can step on it, and step over you, to get ahead of you. No matter if you have the talent, or what you have been through. Generally speaking, teachers want the posh kids to have the posh careers, and the poor kids must take what they can get. Anything else is rare. One gets bombarded with:

"Don't change the order. Don't try to be better than what you are. Don't rise above your station. Who do you think you are? Do you love yourself?"

Jasmine Rose:

It doesn't make much sense that people so love a Cinderella or rags-to-riches story. It has to be in the media, or in a book, or on TV first. THEN people love it. But not in their daily life. If you are not to 'be better than what you are' what would they want you to be? A broken-down wreck in a rubbish bin that they can feel superior to?

I think that what you are doing is perfect. Rising above it, and trying to make a difference for all the millions of suffering children and survivors out there. But the response you get is doors slammed in your face! When all you want is a little social justice and to help others...

They quickly fall back on their weak colluding policy of 'If you don't have something good to say about someone, don't say anything'. Your mission ruffles feathers and disturbs their 'quiet life'. There are Name-and-Shame Lists for the predators, but the colluders should be named too. I am composing a very LONG Name-and-Shame list for all the people who have not helped, and made things more difficult for you on your journey!

But for a little while there at the Pretoria Dance College I felt that I was seen, and my true worth realized. I was cast in main roles. It was satisfying to be the muse to the choreography of the teachers and lecturers. The head teacher created a role on me in a Neo-classical Ballet and Contemporary Fusion piece telling an African tribal story. The African Princess heroine saves her lover and gets turned into a tall-standing ant heap. It was written into the choreography that I would scream when the *Sangoma* (witchdoctor) casts the spell on me. I was very keen to scream. I needed to primal scream. I had a few practices. It was good. But the choreographer decided, without trying it out first, that I was too shy and would not be able to scream loudly enough. She taped herself giving a pathetic whining scream instead! As you can gather I was rather miffed and thwarted. I needed to primal scream. Nevertheless, the piece was a great success and was performed in Pretoria and at the Grahamstown Festival. Bliss.

But by the second half of the year there was trouble. My parents couldn't pay for my fees, so my father went to speak to the head lecturer and I was offered a bursary. I could breathe again – but I was slipping back into the less worthy scholarship girl status… I felt the pain, but donned

In the Wings

the mask and kept on dancing. And as I danced Tom became more obsessed...

I noticed that people were noticing his inappropriate behaviour, but nobody did anything. When I was in my late twenties (a decade later) one of the lecturers told me that they had all suspected the abuse but didn't know what to do about it. They thought something was wrong, but they weren't sure...

People (even abuse victims) often ask me: What is abuse? Here is a table of words that come up on thesaurus, and a few I added in myself:

Misuse	Mistreatment	Swearing	Ill-treat	Insult	Exploit
Exploitation	Cruelty	Name-calling	Mistreat	Swear	Misuse
Manipulation	Ill-treatment	Invective	Mal-treat	Shout/hurl Abuse	Manipulate
Mis-handling	Violence	Insults	Molest	Call names	Exploit
Mis-application	Maltreatment	Verbal Abuse	Batter	Use foul language	Take advantage of
Taking Advantage of	Neglect	Foul Language	Hurt/harm/injure	Denigrate	Subjugation
Using badly	Exploitation	Demean	Treat badly	Be-little	Dominate
Oppress	Bully	Mental Harm	Be violent towards	Humiliate	Inappropriate obsessive control

This is what I was dealing with on a daily basis. I was not alone. There are billions of us being treated like this by individuals, groups, organizations, institutions and governments. We are surviving the 'Nasties'.

The better I did in my dance career, the more violently controlling my father became. When I was in training in Pretoria I was invited to guest perform with the professional company in Durban. This would have been a huge honour and great first step for my career.

My father stormed into the rehearsal and removed me practically by the scruff of the neck, feet dangling in the air. I knew how the Jews must have felt when the Gestapo arrived to arrest them.

He ranted at me, grabbing and bruising my arms, swearing that he wouldn't let me go because, "The fucking male students would try and get into your pants". Reasonable behaviour for a father?

Jasmine Rose:

Line from the film Larry Crowne*:*

"I'm just a guy, who's a guy, being a guy"

Your average father might read that individual story and say that he was entitled to react that way. So much of what Tom did was passed off by others as him 'just being a protective father'. He was forever trying to pull that con on me too. I remember him telling me in gritty detail when I was only five years old, that if anyone were to try to harm me while I was playing in the garden he would leap out of the window and save me, even if he only had his underpants on.

In the Wings

This was a performance for my mother's benefit too and he would put on similar acts for others. She didn't seem to notice his completely inappropriate stressing of his underpants and state of undress. But I remembered. It did not make logical sense and I knew that I was in dire need of protection from HIM!

He still constantly, deliberately messed up my relationships with other people. If anyone became too helpful or supportive towards me he would remove me or cause a problem. He didn't allow me to be alone with other people much. He was always prowling and lurking.

I was still in my slave/prisoner alienated role. There were invisible chains and a trained act that I had to perform on pain of death.

This is what people struggle to understand. The victim is a hostage under constant threat even though they can't see the handcuffs or chains. Like that poor girl in America who was abducted as a young girl and then kept in the backyard with the chickens as a sex slave, forced to have the paedo's children with his wife's full knowledge.

People actually had the cheek to judge the poor girl and say, "Well, if she was really a prisoner why was she seen in public with him a few times?" Stop and think before you speak people. She was clearly under threat her whole life and too terrified to do anything. Terror and doing what you need to, to simply survive, becomes a way of life.

Jasmine Rose:

Completely pisses me off how people judge the victims because they don't have the balls to confront the perpetrator! Nobody is immune from being a victim.

There are predators in society on every level, in all walks of life and everyone needs to wake up to that fact. People are wandering around like a herd of half-blind sheep, and instead of helping the victims they turn on them and go, "It happened to you because you're baaaaaaa-d!" Jeeze – she gets judged for being a 'free range chicken' occasionally instead of a battery chicken 24/7!

My mother was all excited about being near the Part-time Study University and made herself absent through study again. Nose poked into book. She was hiding behind her qualifications and her study, so that she could avoid the fact that she was avoiding the disaster in her life and mine. The Academic Avoiding Real Life syndrome. My brother was away at boarding school.

I was alone.

Ballet Pole Dance

I was chosen by the Head Lecturer to do the launch of Beautiful *perfume by* Estée Lauder *in the function suite of a main shopping centre. This was an exciting, thrilling honour, dampened by the fact that Tom insisted on coming along to do the lighting and sound.*

He prowled around the luxurious carpeted function room. The 'Don't mess with my daughter', alpha-male vibes were bouncing off the ornate walls to such an extent that I was worried the chandelier might fall down!

These vibes were mostly directed at my dance partner, Steven, who was a very virile and straight Alpha-male too. Steven was definitely attracted to me (as he was to most of the female species) and the combination of doing a romantic pas de deux *with me, plus all the dressed-up and perfumed older women watching us, clearly excited him. Gigolo MILF dog that he was. Bless him!*

I was wearing a beautiful feminine costume with a long translucent flowing skirt and flowers in my hair. I enjoyed the swish of the skirt as I twirled and floated around the room. Towards the end of the piece I was lifted up high above his head and then brought down in a romantic embrace, legs around his waist...

This is when it dawned upon me that his jockstrap was not sufficiently restraining his massive hard-on! I spent the rest of the dance holding out my skirt, bobbing and weaving in front of him to try to hide his embarrassment. Not that he was all that embarrassed, mind you. I think that he enjoyed showing off his manhood. Great marketing strategy for further MILF liaisons, no doubt!

Tom noticed the Pole Dance and was supposedly amused, retelling the 'Raising of the flag' tale to family and friends, but he became even more aggressive and possessive. It was like living in a pressure cooker. Violence was on the agenda.

He punched me in the ribs to ensure my full co-operation and servitude in the home. I was dancing the African Princess-turned-ant-heap role and every time I had to be caught by my dance partner I winced in pain. My father insisted that the injury had been caused by the dance. I remember accepting this, and convincing myself that the injury was just a dance injury and had nothing to do with Tom. For my survival I had to do what he insisted – even to the point of distorting reality inside my own head. He never took responsibility for anything, and we all had to act out lies, even within ourselves, to preserve his version of the truth. He had the emotional control of the psychopath. My mother had explained to me that you could tell that he was sociopathic, rather than just having rage issues, because everything was done in a premeditated, planned way and manipulated so that he would get away with it. Like injuries in places that are not easily seen by others.

For my Final Exam choreography I created a piece called 'Solace'. Set in the twenties it was about a *ménage à trois*. Boy and girl happily in love, but a tarty flapper comes along and messes it all up, stealing the boy away and the heroine is left to drink, finding solace for her sorrows in the wine. Prophetic. At the time I only drank the odd glass of wine with the family and never went on student drinking binges, but eventually I was to come to depend on that glass of wine to cope – as us survivors do. It is very hard not to rely on something like that when that is the only comfort left to you...

STARTING AGAIN IN SCOTLAND

Reflections on a Potential Edinburgh Festival Debut Gone Wrong:(2008)

We imagined appearing in dark, subtle lighting – maybe some Celtic Goddessy music wafting - creating a beautiful tableau of the female form in all its fertile glory. But as I saw more blurb and ads about the show I was thinking of volunteering in, and heard more of the buzz it was creating, I had a little rethink...

This was a feminist, supposedly women-empowering stage performance, sold with the benefit of making women feel confident within their bodies. It sounded great and I thought it might be good to add to the piece by standing as a survivor, and my friend thought that it was a nice idea to stand as a breast cancer survivor showing her one remaining breast. What an interesting debut it would be for me on the Edinburgh Festival Stage!

This 'empowerment' apparently required women to take their clothes off. As time passed I realized that the piece was to be marketed with a photo of female headless torsos with their vagina shown exposed centre-front. Wow! Get a bunch of stooges to volunteer to take their clothes off with a fine con job of making them feel empowered, when it is actually about getting audiences in, and making the Director more infamous for getting people to take their clothes off on stage than she already is!

I had been intent on at least going to a rehearsal but I was sent the link for the choreography on Youtube *a few days later and having viewed it I was SO glad to take the advice of the only video comment which was: Don't do it!*

The poor women on the clip were obviously taking themselves very seriously but looked hilarious. They had their clothes on for the choreography clip but if you were to imagine it nude, it could give you nightmares for a week. They were marching up and down with their arms thrust up in a Nazi-type fashion, then bouncing, gyrating, pelvic thrusting and boob waggling at the audience in the most unsubtle way imaginable. It's a wonder the women didn't knock themselves out with the amount of porno, titty-shot bouncing they were forced to do. Dire and degrading! It would be plain painful to perform if you were menstruating or ovulating. So much for awareness of the female body.

Another woman jumping on the bandwagon to use, objectify and degrade women while selling it as empowerment, sisterhood and body awareness! A man friend who saw it said: "All they still needed to do was turn around and waggle their bums at the audience, spread wide-legged and do the old cancan forward bend to show the audience what they've got."

Consumption of alcohol was also encouraged in the marketing. Have a drink ladies, lose your inhibitions to get the audience in, who can also get drunk and lose theirs. WTF? The audience was well filled by the Mack Brigade and the 'Lezbe Friends' fraternities.

The misuse of gullible volunteers is performed in the name of Art on the Fringe! Of course, the City of Edinburgh makes mega-millions from the Festival but the poor artists are left starving and struggling in the wake of it all...

Is this another thing that should change as part of the New World Order?

Jasmine's rant:

Just thinking about it makes me feel like the embodiment of the Three Furies! Women acting like men and driving other women to drink! Candy makes you randy, but liquor is quicker.

In the Wings

As old Bernard Shaw said: "Dance is a vertical expression of a horizontal desire." Ha, ha! I know I have hit on your pet hate there...

Do people understand the concept of a Professional Dance Artist who actually does that as their job, gets paid properly, and doesn't have to moonlight with all kinds of 'other hidden activities'? Like selling socks, pole dancing or being 'nice' to fans?

Never mind the Value the Arts campaign – I want to start a Value the ARTISTS campaign!

The story continues...

Denise Stephani

EXT. VALENTINA'S HOME - DAY

Valentina arrives home - still stamping out her new 'Fugly' dance - but with more lightness and humour now. She stomps and twists up to the blue door.

The ground floor council flat is a splash of colour in a grey depressing block. The guttering and window frames have been painted vibrant colours - a rainbow mural on the wall. There are colourful flowering plants on the window sills. It brightens up the dull day.

INT. VALENTINA'S HOME - DAY

Valentina waltzes into the lounge - to the sad, glum faces of her parents.

>   FATHER
> They're sending us back.
>
>   VALENTINA
>   (Distraught)
>   No! They can't. There is nothing
>   there! I will never be able to
>   dance professionally...
>
>   FATHER
>   There is nothing we can do. We
>   leave next week.
>
>   MOTHER
>   They educated us British...
>   Europeans came and took - created
>   class systems and wars to take our
>   things - divide and conquer - but
>   when we need safety we are not
>   British enough...
>
>   VALENTINA
>   We will have to...
>
>   (BEAT)
>   build Rwanda again.

INT. SUSAN'S LOUNGE - NIGHT

Susan sits in a red silk gown in front of the telly, leg up, in plaster, watching Britain's Got Talent. She pulls a blonde wig on her head and sensually applies red lipstick. Her red feather fans are on the coffee table in front of her.

(CONTINUED)

In the Wings

CONTINUED:

INT. JOHN'S KITCHEN - NIGHT

We see the Job Seekers form on the table - but John tap-dances in front of Britain's Got Talent, strumming his banjo, ending with a flourish and a bow to the panel.

INT. LOUNGE IN A YOUTH-AT-RISK SHELTER

Morag smokes a fag in front of the telly, secretly sips at a bottle of Alcopop, and gives Simon Cowell the finger.

INT. PASSENGER JET - NIGHT

Valentina sits in a row with her parents watching Britain's Got Talent on the central aisle TV. She turns her head and looks out of the window at the dark night sky.

EXT. MAGICAL STARRY SKY - NIGHT

MUSIC:

>   VALENTINA
>   (mouths the words)
>   Aah starchild, things are gonna get
>   brighter...

Valentina flies out of the window - up impossibly high. Eyes gazing upward... Arms raised in a V... To dance among the stars.

                                                       FADE OUT.

Chapter 9

Ballet Company Bollocks

Afrikaans saying: *So gemaak en so gelaat staan*

Translation: This is how I'm made and this is how I'll stay.

STARTING AGAIN IN SCOTLAND

North Berwick, *Blenheim House Hotel*

Having contemplated the glorious view since sun-up from my room window -scribbling away and inspired – I decide to take a break and get out into the fresh air.

I stamp across the beach looking down at the colourful stones.

So many bright colours - pebbles rounded by the currents of the sea. It must be like a rainbow under the water to be able to produce so many different coloured pebbles.

The white seagulls swoop overhead and plunge down into the sea – shooting up again with their treasure: Silver wriggling fish. A boat chugs out in the bay, men drawing up cages with crayfish. Food from Neptune – a treasure for humans.

Bass Rock looms out of the mists – powerful and stately. It wears its history with pride. I am having an affair with the sea. I am so in love with it. I don't know why there is a Nature/Nurture debate. It is Nature that Nurtures.

I trek past the Seabird Sanctuary and sea pool, heading to the far side of the bay.

In the Wings

I have my eyes set on Jacob's Ladder.

A stairway that climbs the sea cliff and gives an expansive view over the bay.

White seabirds float on the bay and from time to time they rise up and sparkle in the sun like pale confetti, lifting and twirling in the wind... or a flurry of snow in a swirling upwind...

or angel feathers...

Maybe they are watching me as I watch them and are willing me to write –

because the survival of nature depends on voices like mine...

As I climb, I think of the scaling of heights to the heavens and a greater understanding of life and the universe. I trek up to a bench to rest, and there, standing out brightly amongst the dark green sea grass and bracken is a bright bunch of yellow roses.

It must have been someone's special bench.

I meditate on the ocean and flowers and, feeling refreshed, I meander down to the town.

I pop into both confectionery emporiums, steal some deals from the *Thrift* shop and find a posh jacket in a charity shop for dirt cheap. This is heaven.

It gives me blessed rest while I contemplate the painful secrets of my life, and how the difficult sacrifice of revealing them could help heal the world...

Denise Stephani

Botticelli's Venus

The first role I danced for the Ballet Company was actually before I got into the company. I was asked to choreograph and perform a piece on the theme of Botticelli's Venus.

It was the launch of a Minolta *photocopier machine with the word 'Pearl' somewhere in the name and marketing. A huge oyster shell was built. Amidst lots of hot-ice mist, the shell would open and I would emerge like Venus... Aphrodite – Goddess of Love.*

I would waft my arms delicately, whilst the production manager crouched beneath the shell with a fan, to blow my hair about like the angel spirits of the wind do in the painting. I would sink down and disappear again into the shell and leopard crawl out of the hole in the back. Only to emerge from the back, twinkle-toe a little more, then return to open up the shell. I would pull the shell apart from each side to reveal the photocopier. My instructions were to whirl about flinging paper all over the floor and in the general direction of the enthralled audience.

What a palaver to sell photocopiers!

There were trays with oysters and champagne wafted about by waiters. I got adventurous one day and decided to have a go at tasting one, and was thereafter regularly quoted by guffawing entertainment guys:

"Oysters. Not my thing. They don't even have the distinction of tasting like snot!"

We travelled to Cape Town and Johannesburg - father in tow doing the lighting and sound as usual, and making revolting sexual oyster innuendos at every opportunity. I was interviewed by a journalist who started the article with the infamous heading:

'Denise Started Out As a Worm' (Erg!)

The journalist also quoted my father as saying: "Denise is everything a father would want."

Indeed. I didn't really have any other option. I had to be everything he wanted or die.

He would laugh and quote Bill Cosby. "I brought you into this world, and I can take you out!"

But secretly... within my deepest depths, there was a feminine roar. Venus was Rising.

When I got into the Ballet Company Tom was working at the theatre where we rehearsed and performed. This had been his prison warder plan all along...

He tormented me all the time. I couldn't get away from him anywhere. He adapted his times and mine so that we would walk to work together. He insisted that I hook my arm onto his and he behaved like a boyfriend not a father. Even at lunchtimes or tea breaks he would appear. He would often force me to eat with him instead of my friends. He would then drag me off to the theatre rooftop areas to keep him company while he smoked his joints. I would feel the pain in my heart as it dropped into my shoes every time he frogmarched me away from my friends. I felt so lonely with this burden of mine.

The suicide threats continued. Sometimes I wished he would jump off the theatre roof. It would be a blessing for all. He was suffering genuine anguish and despair and needed help, but it was also an attempted manipulation tactic to get me to comply with his sexual demands. He was still coming into my room in the mornings and molesting me or insisting that I go to his bed. He still took me with him to get his drugs and he would hide it on me, so that I would have to take the rap for him if caught.

If I complained he would threaten to rape me, kill me and kill himself. His favourite scenario was to rape me in his car then drive down the highway and smash into a bridge, ending both our lives...

Brace yourself for a Jasmine Rose Rant Supreme:

Just read in Heat Magazine *about men who killed their families because they were in debt. Of course, it could really be because they were scared that other secrets would come out...*

But let's go with the debt theory: How dare they? If you want to top yourself, top yourself – but don't take everyone with you. These men thought that their families were nothing without them and their money. That they would never cope on their own. The arrogance of it!

Yes, it is bloody difficult for women and children to cope or get anywhere on this male-centric rock in the sky, but hey, actually, you know what? We are individuals in our own right – not just extensions of the male ego, his possessions and domain!

On a slightly more understanding note: Shame, poor guys - think of all that pressure they put on themselves by having that attitude...

Firstly, it is so unhealthy to equate success and love with what you own. For your whole life to be linked to material gain is not good. That is the First World Dis-ease which is causing so much stress, illness and suffering. We need to follow the example of countries like Bhutan which apparently has a Gross National Happiness Index as part of its social system.

And if the dear chaps would stop putting themselves in the position of God over everyone they would feel so much more relaxed and happy. It is terrible for them. It is an inequality that men are suffering from. I would love to invite them to be equal to me. We need to celebrate the differences which COMPLEMENT each other, and create a unified whole.

A matriarchal society makes so much more sense and would fit in so much better with the natures of men and women. Women deal with the running of the community and relating, raising the children and making sure that all are fed, clothed and housed. We are good at that. Dominating males clearly suck at it. They have proven beyond a shadow of doubt what disastrous leaders they are when left to their own devices! They have driven the world to the brink of destruction.

I bet that the advanced civilization of Atlantis was a matriarchal society. That is probably where the legend of the Sirens comes from. The sailors were terrified of being stranded there and losing their powers and domination over women. They were scared of being emasculated. Like the Samson and Delilah story. But women are so much more in touch with the Cosmic, the Divine and the Greater Good. We know this. Equal power and say would be good for all, and within a healthy Matriarchal Society that is much more likely to happen. Do you think that we could opt for a Matro-Patro society?

Denise Stephani

When they treat us as less - we wear a mask and smile. Can they not see that we are gritting our teeth like crocodiles? We gaze up at them inauthentically (adoringly, they think). Can they not see that we are rolling our eyes at forty miles an hour in disgust at their egocentric macho-male-bravado antics? Whatever made them think that they are the centre of the universe? That they are closer to God? We are the creators. We carry the flow of creation and generations through us. In the philosophy of duality there is a creator/creature theory. Blokes have turned it all arse-ways making out that they are the creators and we are their lowly creatures. Sorry loves – it just ain't so! The opposite in fact. Males are OUR creatures that we create and bring into the world, who are supposed to be OUR helpmates and a bit of brawn about the place when needed.

Can they not see that we are seething with rage? But we hide it so well that we ourselves don't realize it until much later in life. We've had to hide it, because women who matured into the full realisation of themselves and the World Con got burnt at the stake as witches for hundreds of years.

South Africa is a country that still has witch-burnings and the new favourite – Corrective Gang Rape for Lesbians to 'cure' them of preferring women. Women are terrified and revolted from the abuse of men, and then men want to 'cure' them of wanting to be with a safer partner.

I really don't know how I live and function knowing all this stuff. I want to scream and scream and scream. I am the banshee. The Valkerie. I want to avenge the women and children and Mother Nature. I want to correct the imbalance. How dare they!

The Ostriches would say, "If it ain't broke, don't fix it." But it is broke!!!

The only occasional blessings were tours where he couldn't find a way of tagging himself along. On one of these blessed breaks we went to Bloemfontein, which meant I was about half a country away from him. The relief. But even there his sick influence followed...

It was very obvious to other people in the theatre world that something strange was going on. That there was a mystery. Unfortunately, instead of helping me the rumour was twisted for purposes of jealousy. There were various gossipy rumours going around the company at the time. We finished warm-up class one day and the company management called a meeting in the big rehearsal studio of the *Bloemfontein Theatre*. Everyone was there. The dancers, teachers, director and the technical crew. All together, more than seventy people sitting on the studio floor waiting to hear why this emergency meeting was called.

The management said: "There are rumours going around."

1) Alice is anorexic. (My friend)

2) A married male dancer was caught bonking a ballerina on the grand piano.

3) Denise is having an affair with her father.

To my horror they went on to say:

"Denise, stand up." I had to obey. There I stood, quivering in front of the massive crowd of people.

"Denise is this rumour true?"

I shook my head, 'No' and crumpled back down to the floor.

"Well – you see," they said, "none of the rumours are true, so let that be an end to it!"

I could see that many were shocked and felt bad for me, but there was a bit of Schadenfreude too. I think a lot of people guessed at the abuse and could see that I was terrified and traumatized. I often had tears running down my cheeks as I did *barre* training in the mornings. I would normally cry through pliés, tendus and ronde de jambs and then managed to pull it together by centre-work. I am sure that people saw. Management must have had a reason for using my story for their purposes instead of having compassion for me.

So I was even more stuck, with no help. I had denied it publicly even though there was some truth to it, but I couldn't explain that I was not a willing participant, and was fighting hard against it every day. I wanted to cry that I was exhausted from fifteen years of battling and resisting and fearing for my life. If someone with a kind heart had taken me aside privately and asked, I could have, but nobody did.

Tom laughed at me when I told him what had happened and asked him to act in a more normal and appropriate fatherly manner. He felt nothing for my pain and humiliation.

Jasmine Rose:

In a tribe or community in the past, Elders would traditionally have spoken up and intervened. But the dominating First World has done away with that, and made sure that people are isolated and unsupported. If the Third World is now to be called The Developing World, then the First World should be called The Deconstructing World. Lots of ugly construction and total social destruction!

So a few weeks later you stood on the roof of the theatre, on the very edge - contemplating jumping and suicide. You nearly leapt - but changed your mind. What were you thinking? What changed your mind? Oh yes, I remember now – you told me...

You thought that many of the theatre staff would come up with some cocked-up theory about why you had committed suicide. The gesture wouldn't be worth it. Many would be highly titillated and you would have had to haunt the damn theatre for the next 1,000 years just to get some kind of justice or truth! Better that you decided to stay on with the living to be a Diplomat for the Downtrodden...

So life continued on its merry way...

Galas:

It wasn't all misery. We had exciting Gala Events and the one year we were given an allowance to have an evening dress made up for a stately fashion parade.

Us ballerinas paraded down the grand staircase onto stage and showed off our dresses whilst being led by the men in their posh tuxedoes. It was very over-the-top but fabulous. The newspaper chose five of us to be photographed in the dresses that they found the most interesting. Mine was a Greek Goddess style dress with a flowing satin train that my mother and I had designed and made.

I did have some good mother and daughter moments with her. It is such a shame that the good things were destroyed and cancelled out by the bad. And the brooding possessive 'Phantom of the Opera Stage' was always lurking and watching. Tom took full credit for the dress design, preening and strutting. He made sure that he was constantly at my side so that no-one could approach me or ask me out.

Nutcracker:

I was definitely being noticed. I got a great review for being a drunk aunty in Nutcracker *and even the management praised me for my acting skills. Somehow I got fully into the persona of a lonely old spinster, resorting to the sherry to survive an interminable children's Christmas party. I wobbled and weaved amongst the other 'guests' almost tripping up as I exited full of the party spirits. I sobered up fast and rushed off to do a very quick, quick change for the Snowflake scene. I sparkled and skittered across the stage in my diamante tulle, only to rush off again to don the Sapphire Blue tutu for the magnificent Waltz of the Flowers.*

Jasmine Rose:

That's what the world needs to sort it out. A little bit of nut cracking!

On my twentieth birthday Tom punched me in the mouth because I wanted to go out with Alice (my ballerina friend with the eating disorder) who shared the same birth date.

In the Wings

Portrait in Greek/Roman Gala Dress

Venus Rising?

Mary's monologue afterwards went like this:

"You provoked him. You are stubborn. You must have consideration for the fact that he might have a slight case of angina."

When my friend Helen from Dance College arrived with sparkling wine they sent her into my room, and acted as if it was perfectly normal for me to have been beaten and have swollen, bleeding lips on my birthday. They joked that I could bring down the swelling by putting my mouth against the chilled bottle. There was no consideration for my feelings.

(Even writing this makes me want to die again. Why stay on this planet where people don't have empathy and compassion for each other?)

When I wanted to celebrate with a friend it was a violent 'no', but when I was to be shamed by the arrival of a friend it was a 'yes'. And even Helen was forced into the role of pretending it was okay. Why do these evil creatures get away with distorting everyone's reality and behaviour?

It is perpetuated by that good old 'You were asking for it' chestnut that all females and victims get thrown at them...

Greek philosopher Solon was asked what the best administered state was. He replied:

"It is that where the people who have not been offended exact as much reparation for an injury done to others as they would have expected to receive themselves."

Jasmine Rose:

Lordy, don't get me started on 'asking for it' and 'women's troubles' - or the low conviction rate for rape!

It's practically the perfect crime because the victim gets blamed. If anything about her dress code, location or demeanour is even slightly less than strait-laced and prudish she is said to 'have been asking for it'. Or she is some evil woman wanting to make trouble for the man. Such double standards! Why doesn't that apply to men?

Imagine the scenario: "You got mugged and beaten up? Therefore you must have 'been asking for it'. Wearing a kilt were you? No pants underneath and letting your goolies hang low? Definitely asking for it!"

So if a girl gang of Ladettes who have been conned into behaving badly too, see a chap in a kilt, showing too much leg with a knife in his sock, does that mean he is inviting rape? Or to have his bits cut off with the handy weapon? If he drinks a pint too many and flashes his bare arse in public does that mean he is inviting a swift bit of justifiable sodomy?

What about those creepy uncles who wear baggy shorts with the trouser python sneaking a peek at the hem? What are they asking for? What crime can we perpetrate upon them and walk off scot-free for? The answer to THAT would satisfy my need for fairness.

I wasn't even allowed to keep my birthday presents. A male dancer who liked me gave me a beautiful pair of classic diamante earrings, which were perfect for wearing out, or on stage. Tom hit the roof. He forced me to give the earrings back to my disheartened swain.

The prison sentence continued. Tom even told me what to vote.

(Although I secretly voted differently. Minor rebellion.)

My mother voted what he told her to. Now that women have the vote, do we really have it? The slave-masters tend to insist on grabbing those extra votes from the females in the clan.

My parents moved out of the flat, to take jobs in Tzaneen near the farm, but he would still phone all the time, just arrive, or do creepy silent calls to check up on me. I wondered if God was watching too…

Jasmine Rose:

Yeah. That's all you needed. Another stalker! Ha ha!

Basement Church:

When I joined the Pretoria ballet there was a posse of Reborn Christians who attended a popular church movement with a famous reformed gangster.

One of the keenest members was an over-energized male dancer who later became a missionary. The same Cocky Rooster that I wrote about earlier. Us newbies were to be his little Christian Chicklets. He would call meetings and peck and prod at us, forcing us to 'speak in tongues' in the theatre basement. We were performers. We were able to oblige him.

But we did have moments of genuine spiritual connection. Stage fright and pre-performance nerves are a bit like a near-death experience. Very high quality prayers go out just before you step out on the boards and you feel that connection very profoundly.

Jasmine Rose:

Who is God? Is He this great big scary father figure in the sky that we have to beg, placate and plead with? I don't think so. All the begging, placating and pleading doesn't get very impressive results. The empirical answer based on scientific assessments and results would have to be NO.

For thousands of years we have lost track, and lost the truth. We had it more right in the age of Goddess worship, but even then a part was missing. We have been wandering around in the mists getting it all wrong. And the Universal Mind has given us as a human race the free will to do that.

But the problem is that the free will of some has destroyed the free will of others, and is now endangering the survival of the human race and all nature as we know it on our planet.

I think that if God were to choose a form, it would be as a sweet, creative little girl. I think that if God had choice and had not given over free will, the whole planet would be run like a precious little girl would run it. Little girls – before they are distorted by the world - simply love beautiful things, love nature and want to play and have fun. Girls just wanna have fun! *by Cyndi Lauper is God's prayer for the world. It is the unchecked testosterone that distorts and destroys the beauty and causes hardship, suffering and wars. Boys who kiss the girls and make them cry.*

Come play with me. Imagine God as a lovely little girl, a bit lonely in creation, deciding to create a system of nature with a few populated worlds. A bit like someone with a collection of dolls' houses or Lego *sets... But these places have an inner magical energy. They develop and evolve themselves and are forever doing something new and entertaining. They go off track but ultimately the Kind Creator brings them back to the original quality of Goodness and Love.*

Before any decision is made, we should ask ourselves – what would a mother think and what would a little girl think? Little girls are often very mature and maternal. They take on big responsibilities at a young age. They play housie and act the mother role from two years old already. They are the wise ones. So many disastrous decisions are made because these crucially important majority voices are not heard, or even considered.

To fix all the problems within all the systems, economy, nature and Unfair World Order these voices need to speak up. The Community of Humankind needs to tap into the inner voice of the Little Girl Mother to heal the world. "Suffer LITTLE GIRLS to come unto me, for theirs is the kingdom of heaven".

I know. Completely the opposite of what we have been taught by all the bloke-distorted scriptures. It is so important in life to be WILLING TO BE WRONG. And maybe we as a human race are being confronted at the moment with how wrong we have been. Maybe what is right is completely different to what is happening now and EVERYTHING needs to CHANGE. We all need to do something different. FAST!

Or am I just farting against thunder, people?

Interesting theory Jasmine! For that to work we need to drop the 'rose-coloured spectacles' and 'remove the scales from our eyes' and make a proper effort to see what is wrong in the world. It is actually less depressing than pretending, especially if you then take action. Depression is suppressed anger and action. Taking action for positive change is good for mental health. Then you don't have to croon the 'Pretender' blues!

One of the problems that we have with women taking action is the maintaining of the 'I am too ladylike to know such things', naïve stance. Especially of the generation born before the seventies…

Reminds me of a lovely story one of the corps de ballet *dancers told me about her mother:*

Louise's mother suffered from headaches. She was concerned about taking too many headache tablets and was trying to find an alternative cure. The two of them went into a chemist across from the theatre. Louise went to ask the chemist for advice and, as they made their way back to consult with her mother, they saw her standing next to a display holding a long, gently vibrating penis-like object against her temple, thinking it was a massage cure.

She had unknowingly found the sex toy display, because she was far too ladylike to know!

That's one way to cure a headache…

Ah, *Die Mense.* (The people.) In Afrikaans there is a saying: *Jy hou jouself dom.* Translation: You keep yourself stupid. It is used to describe people who deliberately don't inform themselves. Handy phrase to describe those who simply have no intention in hell of changing or doing.

Tom often used to say: "*So gemaak en so gelaat staan*". (I was made this way and this is how I will stay.) One of the things that stops *Die Mense* from creating positive change is the fact that they are working so hard to preserve an image. Unfortunately the image depends quite heavily on not admitting that anything horrible has ever happened to you, or that anything is wrong with the world.

I have often felt like my very spirituality and personality and everything has been attacked by *Die Mense* because they can't handle the simple fact that Bad Things Happen to Good People. This problem has arisen time and time again, right from when the nun told me that I 'had the devil in me' when she found out what my father was up to. According to her thinking, if I was a 'good little girl' I would be on the hotline to God and then nothing bad would happen to me. The fact that I was a victim of horrible acts meant that I was bad. No wonder religious institutions are a hotbed of un-confronted secret sin.

Jasmine Rose:

The Dalai Lama went through hell - and Mohammed, Ghandi and Jesus and all the great teachers. They spoke up and jumped up and down. They tore the curtain of the Temple etc. and they are revered. Can you imagine saying to Jesus – Yeah but you got pinned to a cross, therefore you must have been bad, or been thinking negatively and created it as a lesson to yourself. Or – ha ha! How about this: You have bad karma from a previous life. Or, your prayers were obviously inferior, so you deserved it. Or, it's all just part of your 'soul university' course, so 'let go' and 'move on'.

The same applies to saying that kind of nonsense to starving people in Africa, and the millions of poor women

In the Wings

who have been genitally mutilated, raped or stoned to death under false charges. Or the child slaves in India and Pakistan, or survivors of war and genocides.

Afrikaans saying: *Nou is ons in die **kak**.*

Translation: Now we are in the **shit**.

There exists some concise Urban Wisdom which is all over the Net and on mugs, T-shirts etc. It is a brilliant breakdown of the majority of the world religions'/spiritual paths' reactions to Shit Things Happening to Good People.

Here it is with an African Twist:

Taoism: Kak Happens.

Hare Krishna: Kak Happens Rama Rama Ding Ding.

Hinduism: This Kak Happened Before.

Islam: If Kak Happens Take a Hostage.

Zen: What is the Sound of Kak Happening?

Buddhism: When Kak Happens is it Really Kak?

Confucianism: Confucius Say - "Kak Happens".

7th Day Adventist: Kak Happens on Saturdays.

Protestantism: Kak Won't Happen if You Work Harder.

Catholicism: If Kak Happens, I Deserve It.

Jehovah's Witness: Knock, Knock, "Kak Happens".

Unitarian: "What Is This Kak?"

Mormon: Kak Happens Again & Again & Again.

Judaism: Why Does This Kak Always Happen to Me?

Rastafarianism: Let's Smoke This Kak.

The list is much longer if you *Google* it. What would I add?

African Ubuntu: Don't hate your brother, hate his Kak.

New Age: Kak happens because you created it.

'The Secret' Cult: Kak happens because you choose to create it.

Laws of Attraction Fundamentalists: Kak happens because you attract it.

Karma Freaks: Kak happens in this life because you were Kak in your last life.

Therapists: I've scratched around in your childhood Kak – now let go and forget about all that Kak so that I can feel like I've earned my fee!

I am with the Mystic Alchemists:

"Let's transform this Kak into gold!"

Jasmine Rose:

And, of course, if you try to tell people about your story they say:

Moenie kakpraat nie. *Don't talk shit.*

But here's a different philosophical mind expansion thought...

Why does it not occur to anyone that Buddha, Jesus, Mohammed, Krishna, Aristotle, Da Vinci, Einstein or any of the greats who are expected to reincarnate, might come back as a woman? People would treat women a lot better if that little thought would occur to them. That is just what one of those great men and spiritual teachers WOULD do.

Because they fought for the downtrodden and they were warriors for the truth!

What if God was one of us? Just that lady with her baby and shopping on the bus? Or as the greats taught: What if God was ALL OF US?

Ah, but it doesn't occur to us that we have the power of recreating because we're all more inclined to 'Fiddle while Rome is Burning'. Nowadays it's fiddling with the thumbs on the iPhones to get the latest porno updates, followed by a quick fiddle in the pants!

Denise Stephani

<ins>YINYONA AND YANGAMO SCENE</ins>

EXT. NIGHT - OUTER SPACE - SOMEWHERE IN THE UNIVERSE

A contracting and expanding, swirling vortex of atoms, particles and light - the universal hospital where split atoms are reconnected and reformed and universal healing takes place.

As the movement and TINKLING, SPARKLING, MUSICAL sound grows we become aware of two light particles - circling in an elliptical path - in opposition to each other.

The light with the pinker hue is YINYONA - the feminine, rejected for thousands of years by YANGAMO, with a blue glow - the masculine. She circles and follows, but can never catch up, because Yangamo is accustomed to enjoying the power and the struggle. It is nearly too late for their love to join.

But the healing force of the hospital is strong and a wave of golden light showers them and finally, bit by bit, Yinyona gets closer to Yangamo and catches up with him. Her loving peaceful energy surrounds him.

               YINYONA

           Join with me.

```
                    YANGAMO
    Is it time for Balance and Harmony?
                    YINYONA
         It is time for Unity.
The two lights merge in a vibrant
rainbow-light explosion which gradually
fades down to nothing. The hospital is
no longer necessary. Universal healing
is complete.

FADE OUT
```

This was supposed to be an exercise on subtext with the scenario of a possible love connection, but time is running out for the couple to get together. We were told to think 'outside the box' and come up with something different. I decided to write very simply, the collective feminine subtext within a universal metaphor.

That is: 'Stop messing about and get it together – we could make a good creative team if you would treat females as equals.'

I was reading Deepak Chopra and *The Turning Point* by Fritjof Capra at the time. It is a metaphor which encompasses their messages. Male/Female balance is Right Action and essential for our survival.

Denise Stephani

Denise Age 20
Stage face

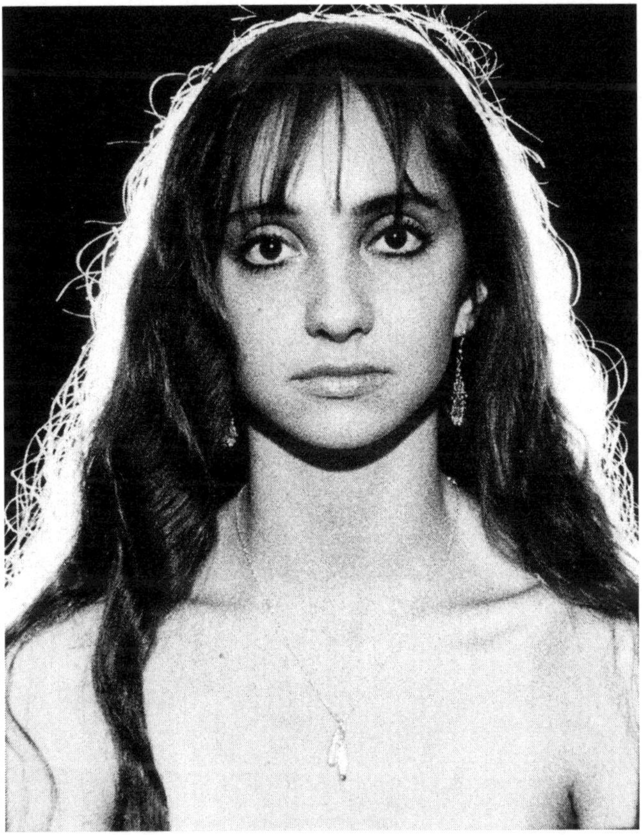

In the Wings

Denise Age 20

Real Face

Chapter 10

Exorcizing the Devil

'Gentlemen don't tell, but Ladies are shamed into silence.' Anon.

Afrikaans saying: *Sy steek hom in sy kwaad*.

Translation: She encourages him in his badness

STARTING AGAIN IN SCOTLAND

Rockville Hotel, Joppa, Scotland January 2012

Have been watching a storm over the Firth of Forth. Exquisite nature. The sea is boiling. Hurricane winds whipping up the waves and spray. The sun glints down on the spray creating rainbow colours stretching across the waters. I have never seen such a magnificent rainbow effect in my whole life, and I am a rainbow watcher of many decades. Always looking for those rainbows - symbols of hope...

The birds love the storm just as much as me, they swoop and spiral and soar – up, up and down, and up again.

And then as the sea mist clears, I see a seabird down below, struggling against the wind and hovering, just over the frothing waves. Flying behind it, like a pennant is a luminous green plastic bag - caught around its leg.

I can see that the bird is exhausted. On the point of collapse.

So tired of having to struggle and strive

and try to survive

> this man-made disaster.

So, Hurrah! The family were gone north to Duiwelskloof, Tzaneen. (Devil's Cliff, how appropriate.) HUGE sigh of relief from me.

They were following one of Tom's Dagga Dreams again. He wanted a farm in the North Eastern Transvaal (now Mpumalanga) so he blew his inheritance from his father on it. To be fair it was a beautiful piece of land on the Oliphants Rivier (Elephants River) near the border of the Kruger National Park. Pristine nature at its best. It sported a wide river with hippos and crocs sunning themselves on the island, lush fertile fields which would be perfect for mango and pawpaw orchards and a *koppie* covered in quartz and fool's gold which glinted in the bright African sunshine...

Which brings me to the problem: It was hot. Salsa hot all year round. *"Blerrie hot"*, as the Afrikaners like to say. Hot as hell.   Pass-out-from-exhaustion-heatstroke-hot. This was disastrous for my poor fair-skinned mother who was extremely heat sensitive and typical of Tom not to consider her, and her physical comfort in all of this. It was also covered in spiders. Poisonous ones. Ones that came out to view the glorious streaking sunsets and jumped a few metres at you! Hardly great for her arachnophobia. But "psychos don't care. They don't care. They don't care. They don't care," to quote psycho-expert Thomas Sheridan in his book on psychopathy, *Puzzling People: The Labyrinth of the Psychopath*.

There was also very little development, as it was the undeveloped half of another farm that got sold off. So - no house. Tom and Mary bought a caravan which they plonked under the spreading branches of a humungous Marula tree. They planned to build a house and develop over several years while my mother worked at Duiwelskloof Hospital and they stayed in the house provided by her work. My brother was sent to agricultural school. He did want to work with animals, but the parents were clearly planning his usefulness around their schemes. Tom's children were not counted as individuals. We were just an extension of himself and all his schemes. His willing slaves. Or not so willing in my case.

I was still getting the same control freaking via the phone, but at least he was far away! The Devil in my life was trying to cause trouble but I forged on. I was planning to buy my own flat using the company housing subsidy scheme and my career was going quite well.

The only problem was that like most young professionals starting out, I needed help from my parents for the approval of the deposit loan from the bank. I could barely feed myself on my salary, let alone save a deposit!

This made me Tom's mistress in his sick mind. His mistress who was going to be housed for his pleasure and convenience, in the flat that HE was buying. The deposit was supposed to be a loan and I would be paying off the flat with my housing subsidy and salary – but as usual he had to have his cake and eat it. He had to manipulate, overpower and master me, and insist that I owe him special favours.

But nonetheless I felt like I could finally breath a bit better... so I advertised for a flatmate to help pay the rent of the flat I was still staying in until I could move to the new one.

In the Wings

Actress Vera moved in with me. She was a student - Jewish Drama Queen from Cape Town. Homesick, missing the same city and both feeling a little lost in Pretoria, we took to each other. She was delighted to be living with a real live ballerina. She was soon bringing friends over and showing off. They all wanted to know what it was like working at the big famous Theatre Complex and being a paid performing professional: "Boot camp," I said.

The company in Pretoria was very strict: on the Russian model. The management were full of B.S. They treated the newest members of the company like dirt. "We will break you to make you," they said. Girly Boot Camp. Of course they did the silent treatment bullying too. They acted as if we were way below them, and would not speak to us in the corridors or the lift if we were polite and greeted them. Then, occasionally, they would suddenly decide to greet you, sarcastically, as if you were rude for not greeting them. Major Mind Games. (Being in the strange Apartheid Regime, we suspected that the dressing rooms were bugged and were very careful about what we said.)

They made you feel like you were nothing and no-one, but I was at least being noticed by fans. Nathan was a fan who came to see each season at least twice. He liked to see the different casts dancing the different roles. He would often sit through a matinée and evening performance all in one day shouting, "Bravo, Bravooo!" joyously throughout. He simply loved the ballet. He didn't care if you were First Cast or Fourth Cast. (Yes, that's right. Ballet has a Caste System too.)

Nathan became rather enamoured of me and sent cards, flowers and little trinket gifts to the dressing room. He kept asking me to join him for a meal between performances. One day I relented and accepted his invitation. It was a good diplomacy exercise for the company for me to encourage him a little, and I felt that I was doing my cultural diplomat bit for a regular client. In the Theatre Complex there were a number of restaurant venues. He took me to the five star 'posh' restaurant with intricately folded napkins, crystal glass and silver cutlery. I enjoyed the sycophantic service from the waiters and the hushed atmosphere. I couldn't eat much because I had to dance later, but enjoyed something small. The company members all had an inkling of it before, but I realized that Nathan was slightly mentally disabled and still lived in his mother's care. That was okay. I was used to that from visiting and performing at the hospitals and institutions where my mother worked. I always treated such people just the same as me. I had a training of 'graciousness to all' that even royalty would struggle to acquire. He told me that he was an assistant hairdresser at his mother's salon, as we finished with a coffee. The poor waiter was very nervous about serving a ballerina, and there was something slightly wrong with the design of the polished silver pot, so he poured half of the scalding coffee into my lap while I chatted about perms. I gritted my teeth and smiled through the pain, in the way that I was trained to. I accepted his profuse, flustered, apologies and scrambled lap mop-up operation whilst steering him away from the private bits. My father had made sure that I was well practised at this.

Then I had to rush off and get ready to don the pink tights, and smile graciously at Nathan in the front row, as I danced with scalded legs!

At the time I had a few male admirers and friends but nothing serious. I was coming out of an isolated terror regime bit by bit, testing the waters of the male domain. Christen, an Australian dancer, was a lovely open, fun guy and we started hanging out together. He stayed in a very posh bachelor pad with a couple of other guys, which had a very nice kitchen and a sauna. We would cook up a storm. The hungry tummy and aching muscles after a day of rehearsals very much enjoyed that experience!

I took the 'hail fellow well met' and 'let me show the stranger around the new town' duties rather seriously, as South Africans tend to do, and we had delightful picnic trips to the zoo, parks, pools, museums and Parliament Buildings of Pretoria. Christen was a gentleman and was happy to be friends, not putting any pressure on me for physical contact – unlike some of the lusty South American chaps in the company who tried to have a go despite being married! Our friendship developed with discussing life, the universe and mysteries. We experimented with telepathy and psychic powers in a small way. He had worked as a chef and we would try out recipes together. One day I sent him to fetch something that was missing from a recipe and while he was out realized that we needed butter too. I sent him a mental message and he got it! He came back saying: "I know that you didn't say you needed butter, but while I was out I felt that we might need it". We were both tickled pink at this proof of our mind powers!

But eventually our friendship did develop and we explored each other in a more physical way. I was very fearful, tentative, repressed and inexperienced. (Behind a bravado act.) But I wanted to know what I was missing. I knew that Chris was about go back to Australia and that he would perhaps be a good, kind and safe person to have a sexual experiment with. There was a sweet, loving feeling between us. In one of our sauna sessions, fuelled by a bit of wine, I admitted that I had never had an orgasm - that I didn't know what it was or how to achieve it. He offered to show me. We moved to his bedroom and he very gently touched me, and stimulated without any penetration, as I requested... until wonderful sensations swept me, and I came. It was a revelation! At least now I had some kind of an idea what the fuss was about, and the attraction with the whole sex business. The mystery of the missing climax which drives people to depravity! I had touched myself occasionally and experimented a little from a young age, since I had been sexualized early by my father's interference, but I had never experienced that peak. A missing puzzle piece to the mystery of life had been found...

Jasmine Rose:

Orgasms - what is that all about? If anything is spiritual on this planet it is the good old orgasm. Yet it is dismissed by the main religions. It is seen as part of an animal urge.

It seems to me that it is more - and has the potential to be very much part of our spirituality. The Vedic, Hindu and Buddhist people have some idea of this, as well as some of the more alternative religions out there. Why does everyone ignore the amazingness of the orgasm? It is one of the real miracles of life which makes life worth living. There are so many miracles that people simply don't value. I mean - what is going on with that? We should revel in the glory of it like a cat enjoys catnip!

With the good old orgasm one feels amazing. It is such a completely different sensation to anything else that we experience in our bodies. It must surely be connected to spirit. It is a connection of spirits! Women have been consistently disempowered regarding their own sexuality and many never have an orgasm in their entire life! What a deep shame. When a woman does orgasm, she feels that cosmic connection in a way that a man struggles to.

(Well – generally speaking men have reduced it to wham, bam and a grunt!) And yet that is where we could work and connect together the best - and end the Gender War.

If people valued, respected and had some good old-fashioned awe for the magic and the mystery of it, it would be more satisfying, and people would be able to stop becoming more and more depraved to achieve orgasms. That would stop them from doing mad things like butt-fucking and donkey punching their own sons, for example. Oh yiss – I know far too much of what happens behind closed doors...

But anyhoo, Denny, you know I also keep on about the Value the Arts *campaign in the UK which is a well-intentioned attempt to help the majority of the ARTISTS who are completely undervalued and exploited?*

Well - I want to start a Value Everything Campaign!

One evening I was leaving to go out with Christen for the last time before he left for Oz, when Vera brought Rodin home. He was a drama student and they were working on an exam piece. I was dressed up to the nines, hair in a French roll, wearing a very 80s tight denim dress with a zip up the front and high heels. Apparently he was smitten.

At that first encounter I was not all that taken with him. He seemed young, spotty and sported a funny, poofed-up, neo-romantic hairdo that required lots of hairspray to keep it up. The expanded James Dean look was very trendy at the time. I had no time for boys, but when he started playing the piano, that got my attention a little.

He became very close friends with Vera and was a regular visitor, so one thing lead to another and we naturally drifted into a relationship. I got the impression that Vera was caught between being pleased that she could please Rodin, who was from an influential Johannesburg family with a well-known actor/playwright father, and feeling miffed that I had stolen Rodin who she probably wanted for herself.

The relationship was a secret. It was my first love and still very innocent and sweet, as we were only at the chatting for hours and making out stage. At sweet 20 I had finally been kissed properly and romantically. Kisses that I could accept and not fight off. Rodin lived in Johannesburg and had to commute, so he occasionally stayed over and slept, very purely, beside me in my bed.

Pretoria Theatre, Wit Wolf Massacre

As a professional dancer, when rehearsing, you normally do class at 10:00am and finish at approximately 5:30pm.

At the Pretoria Ballet Company *we usually finished about half an hour early. If we weren't that busy they let us go earlier. The toes were bleeding and the muscles sore by the end of the day and that extra half hour was usually pointless because when in pain it is very hard to concentrate and think clearly anyhow.*

I was to visit and do a sleepover at my friend and fellow corps de ballet slave, Tatiana, so I had my packed bag with me. We were hoping for an early finish but were ready to catch the 5:15 bus at the latest. However, on this day the Rehearsal Master carried on right up until 5:30pm. We were not happy. There were rumblings of resentment in the ranks. We had missed our bus and now Tatiana's mother would be waiting and not know what had happened on the other side of the bus line where she was picking us up. (Yup – before mobile phones people!)

At 5:30 the management all walked in and told us to sit and listen. Outside the theatre there had been a massacre. Many people had been killed. A white gunman called the Wit Wolf *(White Wolf) from the Right Wing Extremists had committed slaughter on the square. When we went outside we could see the cordoned-off areas and the covered bodies, with markings where bodies had already been removed. There was a shocked hush hanging over the city. We were shaking.*

Where the bodies had lain was exactly where Tatiana and I would have walked if we had managed to catch the early bus as we had wished.

(Another near-death experience to add to my list. Another trauma to add to the trauma list. Yay!)

Around that time I decided to tell Tom that I was seeing Rodin who wanted to go out with me.

Maybe the near-death had awakened the importance of love for me.

Tom's face froze into a grim mask covering his latent fury. He insisted on coming to Pretoria to meet Rodin and have an interview. Tom initiated a heated argument with Rodin about music choices. He hated the fact that Rodin liked reggae as opposed to jazz and blues like him. (Another lovely shaming moment, thank you Tom!) He then proceeded to banish Rodin from the flat and tell me that I was not to see him any more. I was screamingly angry, although it was far too dangerous to let him know it. In my head I sang the same song that I had been singing since I was a little girl.

"Too bad, so sad, my dad, is mad." Sometimes I sang it to a jolly upbeat tune – at other times in a mournful operatic style. This time I tried it reggae style.

Rodin took me to meet his family in Johannesburg. His parents were warm and welcoming. They congratulated Rodin on bringing a 'lady' home. I was very ladylike. My mother, romance novels, school and dance had brought me up to be very courteous and mannered. Clean, well-dressed, well-spoken and respectful. But I worried that if they knew about my father and all that was going on with him, they would want to get rid of me fast. I felt unworthy of being part of such a super family. I was very shy with them because I didn't feel that I deserved their love and kindness. For years I had thought that no man and his family would ever want anyone like me with my background. I felt untouchable.

I was summoned for a visit up at Duiwelskloof shortly after that and I tried to tell Mary and my brother Seton about my love problems and rally their support. Seton opted for safety and adopted my mother's family denial policy by saying, "But that is just a normal behaviour for a father".

Tom's behaviour became more and more inappropriate and insane. He acted as if I was his errant mistress. He kept phoning and checking up on me. I was being stalked by my own father! Everyone around me was normalizing it as usual.

(I can guarantee that the Austrian Fritzl girl could have, and should have, been rescued a hundred times over if people hadn't chosen to turn a blind eye, and lacked moral courage to do or say anything. She should have been rescued when she was a child already – just like me. If my mother had died, that would have been the last that the world would have seen of me. I would have been his prisoner for ever. And no – I am not exaggerating.)

One night when Rodin had slept over, Tom arrived at the crack of dawn. He was there to check up on me. Rodin, Vera and I looked at each other in terror. Oh fuck! We all knew that he would freak. Adrenaline rushed through my veins as I came up with a quick survival plan. I shoved Rodin into Vera's room to hide while I got rid of any clothing or evidence that I had a sleep-over guest.

As I finally moved to open the door which was being banged and rattled impatiently, I spotted Rodin's car keys, cigarettes and ashtray still in the kitchen. I quickly pitched it all into the bin and covered it.

The things I had to do to avoid the rage!

Jasmine Rose:

Okay, suppose you chose your parents like Louise Hay and all these trippy people say... Why would you choose them? A father who kept you under a constant death threat. Decades of torture – mental, emotional and physical. And a mother who was quite happy to leave you in that situation.

Why would you choose that? Why would you want that 'life lesson'? What would that do for the 'development of your soul'? Maybe it is just the luck of the draw and the choice of the straw. Some soul had to go into that little baby body – maybe it was just bad luck? Like stepping on a banana skin. You've lived most of your life with one foot in the grave and the other on a banana skin. Or perhaps that baby body was chosen out of compassion for a greater good? To be a person who gains knowledge and helps the world stop the Culture of Abuse that is making everything ugly...

What is the point of them spouting on about purpose, if they quite frankly don't give a shit about you, and your purpose, and the state of the planet? Or mental health disaster and addiction caused by societal breakdown? They say, "Get real", but they don't get real themselves. They have accepted the news with its daily abuse of women and children reports. War and Nature being destroyed is accepted too. You are 'negative' if you raise awareness.

Why are people so happy to spout those very valid philosophical theories inappropriately? I am not saying that they have no value. I am saying that they have GREAT VALUE - but are far too often used as a weapon to perpetuate denial.

Quite, and indeed, Jasmine, I have experienced much of this.

But in the meantime I needed to stay alive to benefit from this 'education' so that I would live to benefit the world with my experience... I had to come up with a survival plan:

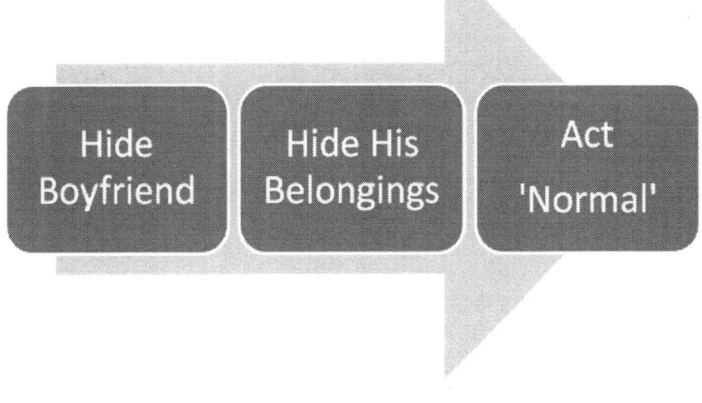

Sylvia – *Cape Town Ballet Company 2003*

In a nutshell, the ballet Sylvia *involves Greek and Roman mythological characters and the storyline is your basic:*

'Boy loves girl, girl captured by bad man, girl restored to boy by god.'

(Lots of drama with the heroine nearly killing her stalking admirer Aminta, at the Temple of Eros. But while looking after him she is captured by Orion, another baddy stalker with an obsession for the below the belt areas. She is finally then saved from a Bacchanalian feast by her hero, Eros and Goddess Diana.)

I was cast in various corps de ballet *roles, but my favourite was the soloist role of a Gypsy Slave. Two Gypsy girls are captured by 'the baddy' together with the heroine Sylvia and taken off to his island lair where they have to dance for their lives and earn themselves a place in the harem. Saucy stuff for the Blue Rinse Brigade who were our main customers... I am surprised we didn't have the odd gentlemanly heart failure. The elderly ladies most certainly waved their fans vigorously and cocked their opera glasses, training them on the virile, masculine, sultan-type baddy with his bare chest and very tight tights.*

Nothing like a good old orgy to get the blood pumping. Many ballets have such scenes and the posh and proper audience members get a fabulous kick out of it. Us dancers rather enjoyed it too. Sexy, raunchy, but safe. Nobody actually sticking anything in anywhere to risk pregnancy or disease. Just a bit of intellectual stimulation. My name means Wife of Bacchus and Goddess of Wine and Revelry – so you can see that I would fit right in!

So, as I mentioned, the ballet was all drama, drama, drama. Sylvia nearly kills her lover Aminta with her bow and arrow, lots of knives waved about for the kidnap and capture, gods and goddesses having tantrums etc. In the midst of it all was a very challenging gypsy duet full of tricks and turns. I had to do a series of fouettés *in the centre of the stage. This required perfect concentration to pull it off, so I hit a slight wobble one performance when I heard a gunshot.*

A gunshot? I knew that this was a dramatic ballet, but I didn't recall that there were guns in it! I went into my usual fear that a radical terrorist from either the Right or Left was sitting in the audience sniping at us. All the wealthy and influential were in the audience and the theatre would be a good place to make a dramatic statement. But no further shooting followed so I guessed that there must be something else happening...

As it turned out it was just my fellow gypsy snapping her hamstring in the middle of a grand jeté *(split leap).*

Yup. Serious injuries are part of the profession. As I finished my turns I saw in my peripheral vision that she had crumpled to the floor and was trying to drag herself off the stage. Oh crap, I thought, there is an audience out there and the show must go on. So I launched myself into the rest of the routine doing her bits and my bits all at once.

I was up and down and all around. I felt a bit like a mad dervish. I have heard of eating for two, but dancing for two is a whole other thing! It may have been easier if I was a quadruped. Although - do you suppose that my legs would have gotten all knotted up and I would have looked truly odd in the dress? Mmm... however, I digress – bottom line is that I managed to finish the dance and the chap playing the Sultan was so impressed that he actually leapt up off his cushions and came to claim me for his harem.

And so he should. I was very good at dancing for my life to please my violent stalker. I had years of experience.

New York City Ballet ballerina, Gelsey Kirkland, wrote her memoir called Dancing on My Grave, *but mine could have been very appropriately called* Dancing for My Life.

So my father tried to kill me. Not the Rodin stay-over and key-in-the-bin time, but a month or so after. After all the years of attempts and threats it finally nearly happened...

which was sort of a relief. When one is threatened with rape and death daily, eventually you just start thinking: So stop threatening and do it already. One just wants to stop dancing and dodging so that the torture can end.

One weekend when he knew that Vera would be away, he arrived at my flat in a very violent and aggressive state. I tried to lock myself in Vera's room but he punched a hole through the door and unlocked it. The phone was in the room so I managed to call my mother and told her what was happening. I said that I had had enough of her husband's crap. She caught a bus and arrived to confront him. It was hours of waiting till she came. I don't remember what happened during all those hours of waiting. The memory is blessedly blanked out.

Jasmine Rose

Abuse is the perfect crime. So traumatic that the automatic brain survival systems kick in, to hide the memories far in the recesses of the subconscious, so that the victims themselves struggle to access full memory of the event! And then it sits there in the background, festering, eventually creating stress-related illness in the body, like cancer. Not just the perfect crime – it is the perfect murder!

By the time Mary finally arrived Tom had taken an overdose cocktail of drugs and a violent confrontation erupted. We tried to call the police but he ripped the phone out of the wall and threw it across the room. We plugged it in, in another room, but he came after us with his razor-sharp hunting knife.

He rampaged around the flat with his glinting knife, threatening to kill us. I ran into the kitchen and grabbed a cutting knife from the kitchen drawer ready to defend myself and save my mother.

It was a terrible and HUGE moment in my life. Even as I write about it now, it feels unbearable. I was so ready to hurt or kill him, if it came down to him or me. Why should I lie down and die? Why should my brother, mother and I not be liberated from this lunatic, even if a desperate act was required to free us?

Jasmine Rose:

And yet you felt guilty for years for even having to contemplate such an action even though he had created the need for it. Why did he not have those feelings of guilt and remorse?

And what about all those out there who rule their families with fear for decades with their knives? Nobody can say anything to oppose them or the knife or gun comes out. It is still very much a part of most cultures. Disgusting!

So I chose what seemed like a better option. I had made sure that the front door, which sometimes stuck, was unlocked and slightly ajar - so when he charged at us with the hunting knife, I grabbed my mother, opened the door and rushed us down the stairs to the downstairs neighbour's door. Thank God they were in, opened the door and gave us safety.

I don't know what I said to them. Probably something like, "My father has gone mad, we need to call the police!" Urgh! It feels so humiliating as I write about it. What must they have thought? Thank goodness they believed us, locked the door swiftly behind us, and let us use their phone to call the police. We must have looked like demented wild women throwing ourselves upon their mercy. I am thankfully blank about anything apart from getting through their door and getting it closed for our safety. Thank God for good neighbours!

Jasmine Rose:

This sort of thing is so common on our planet it is scary. That definitely doesn't make it okay. Millions of women and children are dealing with this kind of scenario every weekend. It is so wrong.

So of course the police came and said that they couldn't do anything until there was 'actual blood'. They told my father to calm down and behave himself. My mother elected to stay but I said, "I am going – I don't trust him." I had called my friend Helen and arranged for us to go to her flat but my dumb, brilliantly clever mother decided to stay. I was not going to go along with her folly. I left under police escort, went to Helen's flat, confiscating his car keys and knife and taking them with me.

My insane mother, Mary, kept insisting on staying with him, despite us all begging her to come with us.

(She was being all forgiving and understanding. That whole mindless, religious 'you have to forgive all' thing has been the bane of my life. It has kept me a victim for decades. Time and a place people! First get all to safety, sort out the problems, THEN consider the forgiveness thing very personally MUCH LATER when you are good and ready!)

Mary called half an hour later, and I could hear that something was going on:

"Your father wants his knife and car keys."

I sensed danger and told her to just answer yes or no.

"Are you in danger?"

"YES."

"Should I call the police?"

"YES!"

He had been strangling her.

Jasmine Rose:

See how adult and responsible you had to be for everyone?

Should you get a medal? Yes.

Did you get a medal? No.

If a male faced the same sort of physical and mental challenge in battle, or on the street, he would get a medal. But because you are a mere female, and treating us like dirt in the home is okay, you had to roll with the punches, shut up, put up and get no recognition for your bravery and courage.

I want to start a Medal and Awards System for Survivors and the people who help them escape!

The police were despatched again, finally got the gumption to forgo the 'Boys Club' and arrested him. This was because he got even more melodramatic and tried to resist arrest by jumping to his death. Unfortunately, and typically, he survived just fine. Hardly a scratch despite leaping out of the second floor window.

Jasmine Rose:

Why do the monsters in the horror movies live on and on? Why do they get the luck?

It's like Freddy and Jason from the big horror flicks. Their damn luck lasted for endless movies. Why do the evil, messed-up, toxic, harmful people survive on and on? It's a hectic message and brainwash: 'The meek shall inherit the earth – but only after the un-meek have messed it up completely and left a pile of bodies.' Is art imitating life or is life imitating art?

So this time the police arrested him 'for his own good' so he wouldn't harm himself. They wouldn't arrest him for OUR good and to prevent OUR harm, but they arrested him for his own good. Something wrong there – don't you think? But anyhow, at least - after decades of bad behaviour in public and private – Tom was finally incarcerated.

So I saved my mother. Helen (brave little soul that she was too) went and got my mother. Helen gets Brownie points in heaven from me. Sadly we are no longer in contact but still I love her dearly for her help and kindness at that difficult time.

Jasmine Rose:

I'm quoting fabulous Julia Quinn and Lady Danbury again: "Us women need to stand up for each other because it is clear that no-one else is going to".

I had to go through the painful process of hiding out at Helen's Aunt's house for the night. Urgh. So bleeergh. Shameful. I truly have had my ego thoroughly smashed by life.

I dreamt that night that I was on a speeding train, and on the train was a psychopath with a knife who was chasing after me wanting to stab me. And then I woke up and realized that I was still in the dream. There really WAS a psychopath with a knife trying to kill me. That awakening was the most painful, horrible moment. I thought that it was all a dream and then I realized that the nightmare was real. Cruel torture. This is the excruciating torture of Post-Traumatic Stress where these horrible scenes are repeated night after night in your dreams. It happens because your brain can't comprehend it, and needs to revisit the horror time and time again, to try to make sense of it. I have suffered this for decades. Repetition of all the gruesome scenarios. Bad enough that it all happened once, but it still repeats on me like a bad curry despite spending a fortune on endless therapies where they promise to get rid of it overnight.

Afterwards Mother Mary said to me: "I am sick of you and your father's dramas". Hello?

The next day I had to go to the police station and lay a charge. Mary sat at my side trying to edit what I was writing. Did she know that my word as a minor (younger than 21) would not be taken as seriously as an adult? She must have. She had studied criminology and sociology after all. Sitting by my side acting like she was supporting, but undermining me all the while!

He was held in jail and not granted bail. He was charged with assault and molestation. My mother made no statements and laid no charges. She left all the responsibility to me. He pleaded guilty to assault but not sexual abuse or molestation. Why would he plead guilty? Having been an ex-cop he knew that if he pleaded guilty, the law of the jail jungle would prevail in prison - the other prisoners would rape him.

My father was pleading his sorry case from the prison to my mother. She went visiting and took him food parcels. Yup – she was one of THOSE women.

But - oh the 'poor me' stories that he cooked up and she ate, even though she knew that seeking sympathy is the classic way that psychopaths manipulate. Oh the crocodile tears that they shed and the hypochondria that they use. Tears and imaginary illnesses to control others.

Jasmine Rose:

"What a pity, what a pity

That the people in the city,

Have a pimple on their titty,

Like a hard-boiled egg!"

Wasn't that the little nonsense poem your mother always used to rattle off to stop you from feeling sorry for yourself? The 'I don't give a damn' poem which left you to bear your cross by yourself. Don't involve me in YOUR troubles.

Good Lord! What was she thinking? Her behaviour was so insane. Taking him snack packs with poison in them would be a more normal reaction! Where was her compassion for you? Or even for herself?

Then there was the ordeal of having to see lawyers with her defending my father every step of the way instead of standing up for us and protecting us. It was hopeless and pointless, and the lawyer saw that, suggesting eventually that I drop the charges. Not a bad decision, since I would have been fed to the sharks in the court, and my mother probably would have lied and testified against me. She was already lying and saying that my brother was emotionally unstable and wouldn't be able to handle it if the truth came out. She was ready to sacrifice anybody to save her hero. I could see the lawyers shaking their heads. Finally I gave in, went to the head magistrate and asked him to drop the charges.

I had a number of reasons for choosing to give up on Justice:

1) No-one was going to help me win this battle.

2) My grandparents or uncle might have helped, but my mother would have disowned me if I told them, and I would probably never have seen my brother again – whom I loved dearly.

3) If it got into the newspapers I would always be known as the Incest Ballerina and would have been famous for that instead of my dancing. It probably would have ruined my chances of ever dancing principal roles. I may even have lost my job as a result.

4) Silence was expected.

5) Justice was unlikely.

6) Nobody cared about the human rights of a white girl in South Africa.

7) I would have been 'burnt at the stake' if I had insisted on being heard and pointed out fault with a man within the Nationalistic White Male Dominated Patriarchal Apartheid Society.

8) Especially an ex-cop and boxing champion.

Skip ahead. So Tom got out after a week. He got a rap over the knuckles from the magistrate who rather classically told him that he was 'acting like a kaffir'. It was pretty amusing that a dyed-in-the-wool racist should be called a kaffir. This was the highest insult in the Old Apartheid South Africa. But I think that the magistrate meant it in the original sense of the word which is 'acting like a God-less heathen', which is not necessarily racist. Just a strong moralistic stance against immoral behaviour - which was much needed in this case.

Tom was released on condition that he had psychiatric help and there was a Court Order instated, whereby I could have him arrested immediately if he turned up at my home and attacked me again.

As part of the Court conditions, we were told to do Family Therapy and an appointment was booked. But my parents manoeuvred a pre-appointment meeting and got in there first, so by the time I arrived, Tom and Mary had convinced the psychologist that I had a Princess Complex and that I was 'making a fuss about nothing'. The first thing he said to me when I arrived was: "Oh, so this is the little Princess," in a sneery, lechy way. So, no help there. How could he be such an idiot and buy it? Why did he not insist on the therapy? I should have had the option of therapy for myself with a female therapist. Something seriously wrong here... A psychologist shouldn't be taken in by a psycho...

Oh yes, that's right. My mother. The psychiatric nursing sister and university graduate: amazing how she studied all the subjects like psychology, criminology and sociology which would mean that she could help him get away with his mad behaviour and block me when I was trying to help her! For years I was trying to save the family and get help for Tom, but she blocked me every step of the way.

Jasmine Rose:

It is amazing what people will do to maintain the status quo...

The psychologist and court never followed up on the case, or made sure that the psychiatric help that the magistrate had ordered was being carried out.

So that was the end of my ambition of owning my own flat. The parents used the money that was supposed to be for the deposit, to pay legal fees and go off on a romantic weekend with a touching reconciliation session of wining and dining under palm trees. I remember my mother waxing lyrical about the whole thing and acting as if nothing had happened, apart from an improvement of her marriage. As if the effects of the event on me were totally unimportant. She didn't even seem to give it any consideration.

She was squeezing her eyes shut and pretending that it hadn't happened. Again.

Jasmine Rose:

I hope that the make-up sex was worth the eternal damnation she may be facing. Although – ha ha! - if hell does exist, she will probably cosy up to the devil and become his top concubine. Old Nick would be just her type! I know that she had Stockholm Syndrome and was trained to kowtow to her captor – but still...

His behaviour WAS devilish and demoniac. Even at the courthouse he gave me a set of steak knives as his so-called 'apology' present. I was devastated and refused to take them. I sobbed, "I hate knives, I hate them! How can you give me knives after what has happened?" He just looked at me with that 'What, me worry?' amused/bemused look. (He regularly used this expression to maximum effect. It was modelled on *Mad Magazines'* Alfred E. Newman character. He was addicted to *Mad Magazines*.)

One minute he was telling Rodin, who was there to support me, that I was 'special and to look after me' and the next he was giving me the psycho keep-quiet-or-else threat-present. And nobody did anything and he got away with it!

What a mad, mad life.

Jasmine Rose:

What was your mother thinking? Was it that old chestnut again: 'I made my bed now I must lie in it' that kept her in the marriage? Or maybe she thought that she couldn't do any better. A lack of options out there...

I saw a great quote the other day:

'Men, even the good ones, are kittle cattle; God didn't give them much sense, and it is a woman's job to make the best of them'. O. Douglas (Anna Buchan, 1877–1948), Jane's Parlour

This question baffled me too. It 'did my head in' to be more accurate. I do recall her spouting the 'bed lying' thing a number of times. But she hated women. She was always on about how women are devious and sneaky, and that men are more sensitive and emotional and better people all round. It was very tough being the daughter of a mother with that philosophy. Of course, now that I am older I can see that she was messing with my mind on purpose because she was jealous about my father's obsession with me - even though she refused to do anything about it. In many ways it suited her to deflect his mad behaviour onto me and let me deal with it – but the green monster resided within her nonetheless... I am sure that Freud or Jung would have a field day analysing her!

Jasmine Rose

Psychology: What is that all about? We all know that women are generally the more emotionally adept species on this planet. Our brains are designed and geared for it. We need to be able to relate to others well for community and child rearing etc. We are the experts on all that. Yet – we have had all these men who have dominated psychology for the last 200 years. When I studied the history of psychology all that I could think was, what a bunch of arrogant, self-important, mentally and emotionally suspect idiots! They all put the psycho into psychology and the anal into analysis!

They have had the odd female assistants to shag and toss the odd bit of credit to, but they as males have lorded it over the emotions of people and ignored the experience of females for hundreds of years.

A lot of these men also came from a country which has a long track record of having a high percentage population of cold, aggressive and pretty emotionless people. How bizarre is that?

The main influence on feelings is men from stoic, famously emotionless Germany?

It's got to be one big hilarious cosmic joke!

What is it with guys that they have had to systematically subjugate and disempower women in ALL the feminine areas of strength? Like emotions, healing, childbirth, sexuality, storytelling, art, spirituality, mysticism etc. Maybe that is why we like to dance. That is one area where most men struggle, and woman tend to be able to excel and stay in charge much more easily...

denisestephani@myspace: When will the world change so that women can stop having to distort themselves? So we can be who we are, and breath for the first time in thousands of years?

Here is a short film script that I wrote when fuming about the futileness of the word 'No' in a woman or child's life.

FADE IN

INT. KITCHEN - DAY

Blonde, blue-eyed ANGEL, washing dishes in steaming water. Looks at her hands.

Her FATHER comes in to check water temperature. Cuffs her across the head. He adds hot water. She shakes her head as the steam rises. Her eyes shine with tears. She looks at her reddened hands.

She looks out of the window and sees her brother playing football with his friends. She sighs at his freedom.

Perched in the corner of the windowsill is CHERUB. She is somewhat unusual in that she is wearing a *Wonderwoman* outfit, but behind her, angel wings spread and glow. The little cherub shakes her head and looks disapproving.

Angel's UNCLE comes in. He leers at her backside. He moves behind her and grabs her backside with one hand and a breast with the other.

CHERUB's face reddens with anger.

INT. BEDROOM - NIGHT

ANGEL is on her bed. Plugged into her iPod. Lost in her world of music. The door creaks open. Uncle comes in. She sees him, eyes widening in alarm. She jumps up and moves to the window, looking out.

Cherub is perched on the windowsill again. This time with a placard on a stick. It has the word NO emblazoned across it in golden letters.

The uncle moves behind Angel and grinds himself against her biting her ear. She raises her eyes and slowly moves her head to the side hopelessly mouthing the word 'no'.

INT. BEDROOM - NIGHT

Angel is moving her head from side to side, dancing around her room, moving and bopping - enjoying a moment of freedom - and then she hears a whistle. Her father's signature call.

She shakes her head 'No' but reluctantly she moves towards the door.

INT. KITCHEN - DAY

She brings a tray of beer and sandwiches for her father and brother. On the tray is a report card to be signed. All As. Her brother's report card is already signed on the coffee table. All Cs and one B.

INT. COFFEE SHOP - MORNING

Angel and her brother serve coffee to customers in a coffee bar. Underneath the counter is an open college book. Angel studies between serving. Cherub sits under the counter, placard beside her, reading the book.

Angel's brother leans on the counter picking his teeth. He glares at the customers and counts out their change - painfully slowly.

INT. COFFEE SHOP - EVENING

The sleazy café owner pays Angel's brother, counting out four ten-pound notes. Her brother shakes the owner's hand, pats his back and swaggers out.

The sleazoid counts out only three for Angel. She starts to say 'no' but he pulls her by the waist to the door, slaps her on the rump and pushes her out. She turns to protest but he shuts the door in her face.

Cherub jumps up and down furiously on the pavement and bangs the NO placard against his door. Angel sadly wanders off.

EXT. CAR - NIGHT

Angel is sitting in a red Ford with her boyfriend MICK. They are making out. Her eyes are glowing with love. His eyes are glowing with intense lust. He reaches across and pushes her seat back.

Cherub marches across the dashboard waving her No placard.

                    ANGEL

  No!

INT. HOSPITAL - DAY

Angel's legs are being pushed into stirrups. She is unnecessarily exposed to give birth. The room is full of STUDENTS and NURSES tutting and judging. Angel covers her face in shame.

Cherub jumps up and down on the DOCTOR'S shoulder waving her placard:

                    CHERUB

  No!

INT. COUNCIL FLAT - DAY

Angel nurses the baby. Mick rampages around the kitchen throwing things out of the cupboard and fridge. He throws his head back and drains the last dregs of his beer. He crushes the can and throws it aside, searching for more.

He looks questioningly at Angel. She shakes her head.

He hits her and storms out slamming the door behind him.

              ANGEL

  No!

Cherub pops up from behind the sofa and swings her *Wonderwoman* rope menacingly.

INT. COUNCIL FLAT - NIGHT

Angel looks out the window shaking her head. Cherub sits cross-legged on the sofa, head in hands.

INT. COUNCIL FLAT - DAY

Angel looks out of the window and at the door from time to time whilst rocking the baby. Cherub shakes her head.

INT. COUNCIL FLAT - NIGHT

Angel struggles in the door with groceries. A teenage, gum-chewing, babysitter rolls her eyes and leaves.

A five-year-old girl sits watching *Barney*.

Cherub lies in a doll's cot on the windowsill. She is sad as she looks at Angel and the little girl. Her placard is bent and out of shape. She picks it up and looks at it. She shakes her head and throws it out of the window.

                                      FADE OUT.

Where is voice of other women in this tale? Even the Angels and Cherubs have nothing to work with, to help from the other side. Why do we just put up with it? The bullies don't respect us for it.

Denise Stephani

Chapter 11

Alpha and Omega

STARTING AGAIN IN SCOTLAND

Scotland is the Land of the Last Witch, and you can feel it. Any outspoken female questioning the status quo or wanting to change this Freemason stronghold can soon find herself 'burnt at the stake' metaphorically - or even literally, since arson is still a favourite retaliation.

I found this information when I was writing in a guesthouse by the waterfalls of Cramond.

The Last Witch – Helen Duncan

The last witch, Helen Duncan (1897-1956), was a medium and the last person to be jailed under the Witchcraft Act. She was born in Callander. In 1941, during the Second Word War, she was 'visited' at one of her séances by the spirit of a sailor who announced that he had just gone down 'in the Barham'. *HMS Barham* was not reported lost until several weeks later, as the Admiralty had wanted to keep the sinking secret. In 1944 Helen was arrested and charged at the Old Bailey under the Witchcraft Act of 1735. She was found guilty and sentenced to nine months in Holloway Prison.

(Christopher Winn : *I Never Knew That About The Scottish*)

I had heard about her previously when I taught near Callander,

at the centre built for the community,

In the Wings

after the Dunblane Massacre.

We wanted to create a performance in her honour.

In Africa there are many witch burnings and killings.

Even animals like tortoises are sometimes burnt as 'witches'

by the same people who pay for witchcraft.

The animal's only real crime is that it can't get away fast enough...

Jasmine Rose:

I shudder at all the terrible things that the dominators have done for thousands of years as they projected all their own evil onto healers and midwives to burn them. Because they can. Silencing and getting rid of the Wise Women makes it so much easier for the evil to continue. Easy-peasy.

I have a pet theory that a high percentage of the shocking number of women burnt, were burnt because they were simply speaking their truth and challenging the status quo. They were speaking of incest, rape, abuse of power and position. They were championing the victims of society and they were blackened, ridiculed and gotten rid of by powerful sociopaths fast. Women, the miracle workers, who are connected to creation and bring life have been blamed and shamed for all, been painted into Jezebels, Delilahs, Magdalene whores and betraying Eves.

'But anyhow, it wasn't a woman who betrayed Jesus with a kiss.' (Catherine Carswell 1879–1946, The Savage Pilgrim*)*

Denise Stephani

If you stop and think for a moment – who has been doing all the evil and devious stuff that has brought massive suffering time after time? Not many women and children – so who? It is the Con of Man which everyone has been buying for centuries. And women have been buying into it and aiding and abetting it too. This is a call for a Lysistrata Revolution ladies! Be authentic and stop rewarding Bad Behaviour. No Behave? No Bonky-Bonky! Withdraw. Boycott.

Men have proven beyond a shadow of doubt that they are not qualified to be in sole charge of this planet. Neuroscience has proven that women have better developed brains with more connections which help with relating and improved thinking. Men know this subconsciously which is why they are always beating down to 'keep us in our place'. Sabotaging, raping, abducting and impregnating to keep us down. It is the time for the rise of the feminine – for the meek to have their needs and values honoured.

It is all a big competitive game to the dominators, but the magnificent French women are all standing up now and saying: "They play and we pay." It needs to be Venus Rising to end the Penis Rising.

All the years my father had called me a witch. He had told me it was my fault that he fancied me. That it was witchcraft. I was the Temptress, Jezebel, Delilah, Eve-like, Magdalene whore. That is how he justified strangling, smothering and beating me. I was a witch that he, as an 'upstanding citizen', had to destroy. Madness and badness projected onto me because he couldn't control himself.

In the Wings

After my father failed to kill me in that overt, knifey kind of way, he found another way of trying to kill me and end my career. A few months later - despite the protection order and interdict, he broke into my flat and scratched around my things, finding the condoms that Rodin and I had left in a drawer. He was livid at finding evidence of my sex life and decided to cause trouble.

Actually up until the whole attempted murder scenario I hadn't slept with Rodin (or anyone) but the fact that I had to escape and live at Rodin's parent's house for a lot of time complicated matters. I felt that I owed it to Rodin to at least give in to his desire for sex for all the trouble and trauma that he was supporting me through. So Tom's act of preventing me from having sex with someone else, actually forced me to have sex with Rodin when I wasn't psychologically ready for it at all.

Rodin and I had been looking after my friend Helen's parents' palatial family home while they were away on holiday. This is where we consummated our relationship for the first time. On the night that it happened we had been to see a sexy cabaret in Hillbrow with songs from the *Rocky Horror Picture Show*. Rodin was in a sulk. Blue balls. A testosteroney Scorpio male watching a famous blonde, smouldering, erotic songstress together with a girlfriend who said she was not ready for full penetrative sex was not a good combination. But the show did get me a bit worked up and horny, so I decided that this night was the night that I was going to end the male sulks and go the whole way.

I had a feeling that I might be about to start my period. I suspected that I wasn't technically a virgin because of ballet and Tom's molestations, but I thought it might be good if some blood appeared. I hadn't told Rodin he was the first man I had properly kissed and made out with, but I wanted him to know that he was the first man that I had willingly allowed into my body. I wanted him to know that it was a special bond that we had. Even if the evidence was slightly skewed.

Jasmine Rose:

"My mother asked a somewhat rhetorical question: How do you keep men happy? You have to feed them at both ends replied my grandmother." Muriel Spark (1918–2006) Curriculum Vitae

What is the big fuss with the whole virginity thing anyway? I think you read too many of those Mills & Boon *romances in the nurses' tea room while waiting for your mom. Originally, back in the bible times, virgin simply meant a young unmarried woman. So if a virgin got pregnant it just meant that she was a young single mom! No shame in that.*

Not that you would have wanted to get pregnant. Disastrous for a ballet career!

The setting of my 'deflowerment' was very romantic and lovely. A beautiful room with gable windows, flowers and candles. We were like a proper Mr and Mrs. I felt like I was taming the beast and that we would have our happily ever after. The sex was uncomfortable and strange the first time, and Rodin was slightly astonished that I had the honesty to admit that, but then we tried again, and it became magical and amazing. Loving sex is so incredible – I don't know why people need to distort it with deviance. Although slightly kinky can be fun...

But I digress...

Tom turned up a few weeks later to ruin things for me. Back in my life and back on form, despite the interdict and court orders. On finding the condoms in my flat he punched holes through them with a thick needle. A week or so later he phoned me and told me what he had done. I was horrified. Rodin and I had used some of the condoms without noticing the holes.

What was the point of this vengeful act? To get me pregnant and make me suffer?

Is that why we have so many teen pregnancies? Sabotage?

Jasmine Rose:

'In days of olde,

When Knights were bolde,

(And plastic not invented)

They tied their socks,

Around their cocks,

And babies were PREVENTED!'

Was he trying to end my career, or maybe kill me with AIDS, or make me suffer some horrible venereal disease? What the fuck was the point of it all? What a total bastard to do that to his own daughter! He knew the suffering, pain and hardship that pregnancy brings – but he wanted to punish and trap me.

Then he insisted on having a lunch meeting. I confronted him with what he had done and told him that I had had to go to the clinic and take the Day After pill which had made me vomit.

He laughed at me like it was a big joke. True Evil.

Of course hearing all this sent Jasmine off into a mega-rant again…

Jasmine Rose:

No apology in sight as usual. Why was this psychopath allowed to operate in society so freely? Why didn't the people who felt something, or knew something, DO something? Or when they did do something, why weren't they heard? The latest statistics show that 1 in 22 people are sociopathic/narcissistic/psychopathic predators who feed on society.

It was, of course, that same old tired thing of: 'If I can't have you then nobody will'. What has happened in this world that men think that they 'have' us anyway? The guy 'gets' the girl. Bloody egotistical, bastards that they are. Women don't naturally go around saying that they 'have' or 'get' or 'own' someone. It is quite simply slavery.

Why don't the retards understand that?

Whenever men do the things they do every day, in every way, big or small, that turns females into sub-human second-class citizens who must 'do' for them and have less equal human rights, they are committing Gender War. There IS a War Against Women. Everyone so smugly says: "Prostitution is the oldest profession in the book." But who normally runs the trafficking, pimping and profits? Not the women who are enslaved. And there have always been more man-whores than girl-whores anyway!

For a man to keep his own daughter in that type of slavery is so wrong.

But if the truth of incestuous family slavery comes out in public, the daughter tends to be attacked and crucified more than the man, because men automatically have the power position even in a simple case of right and wrong, sanity or insanity. It's always the devious witch/bitch woman's fault. And the men run off laughing. Bunch of sociopaths.

What an insane world!

Oh boy – good rant Jasmine! I sure know about that. After all that drama and trauma I was in quite a state. The only thing that kept me going was Rodin's love, dancing and the discovery of the joy of untainted physical intimacy. Rodin was a wonderful lover who knew how to woo and make physical intimacy a special, scintillating experience. We made love all night by candlelight and in between we discussed life, the universe and everything.

We made up funny limericks and wrote scenes for plays and stand-up comedy. He introduced me to Rune stones, and we tried to tell each other's future, throwing the stones to the early dawn birdsong... to see if our relationship would last. I had been through hell for sixteen years, but at least I was finally getting my happy ending...

All was not well though. I kept having the nightmares and vomiting from emotional tension. I couldn't eat and lost weight. Nobody understood what I was going through. Nobody asked for details. At work they knew what had happened and there was an understanding and sympathetic silence.

One of my friends in the company arranged for me to meet the head of Rape Crisis, but I couldn't tell her much. The head shared some of her family traumas, probably to help me to open up, but I quietly thought that it sounded like she had enough on her plate and wouldn't be able to deal with my stuff too. I didn't want to involve anyone who might be endangered. I didn't say anything to my grandparents or uncle. Silence as usual.

I started feeling desperately depressed when I wasn't with Rodin, so I went to the National Counselling Service and the woman there listened to my brief account of the attempted murder and failed justice. When I finished she very brusquely looked me up and down and told me to, "stop wearing black and get on with your life!" No sympathy or invite back. Just an attack on what I was wearing as if THAT had caused all the problems. The usual 'blame the female for what she is wearing' response!

Silence was my safety and sanctuary.

Jasmine Rose:

'Silence is a virtue,

Virtue is a Grace,

Grace is a little girl who didn't wash her face!'

But you know what? Quite apart from any mental health issues, Tom was just a Total and Utter BITCH. Bitchy, mean-spirited and nasty. MEGA MAN-BITCH. Reminds me of that quote I spotted the other day:

'Today I pronounced a word that should never come out of a lady's lips. It was I called John an Impudent Bitch.' Marjory Fleming (1803–11) Journals

They like to call it 'being challenging' but bottom line is that guys, okes *or* manne *are just plain old bitchy, and then they have the cheek to project their crappy behaviour onto us and call us that – plus make us THEIR bitches. So wrong.*

I think that you hold the key to a huge global secret. If people like you started speaking up and being heard and supported the whole World Order would have to change.

'What would happen if one woman told the truth about her life? The World would split open.' (Muriel Rukeyser from 'Kathe Kollwitz' and The Courage to Heal*)*

That could really be a good thing. We could have a fresh start! Draw a line and do something different. Why is that so scary?

Even Rodin had been heartless. A month or so after the event, Rodin tore apart my personality. He said: "You are the most selfish person I know. You give things all the time…"

(I had been very generous with him – put petrol in his car, paid for everything I could from my meagre salary since I was the working one.)

"…but you don't give of yourself," he continued. "You are so selfish with yourself."

Well – hell! Dancing is all about giving. Giving to the audience. Creating a special evening or event in their lives. Performing to raise money for charity. Outreach in the community. Bringing joy, magic and happiness to many! But I knew what he meant…

It was true that I was so frozen with shame that I struggled to interact in the way his family and friends expected. I had been trained to be a personality-less house-slave within our home. Even the ballet world requires silent obeying robots, which is why it made sense for someone as repressed and silenced as me to choose it as a career.

So I suppose those habits seemed strange to his arty, outgoing actor family and friends. I suppose he was frustrated because I was myself with him and his disabled brother, but held back with the others, so they couldn't see what the appeal was. They probably saw my repression and staying out of their way as a kind of superior snottyness. Ballet dancers are often accused of this anyhow. The upright posture doesn't help.

I was just flying under the radar and surviving. I could see that they had taken back their approval of me as his girlfriend now that they knew I had a vindictive, insane, violent father who was a danger to Rodin. Understandably. They knew about the condom episode. His mother had given advice and driven us to the clinic for the Day After pills. But I just needed time and understanding. A little bit of compassion so that I could recover and blossom. It was TOM'S shame, not mine. But everyone looked at me like it was my shame. In books and movies people understand when someone has been through trauma and they help.

Why does it not happen in life?

It seems to happen for animals but why not humans? I am the elephant in the room that no-one wants to talk about. Why is the world so scared of people like me? Why does what we have been through make them lose their compassion and understanding? Why don't people do the psychological maths? Is there a big gap in education? Or a big gap in their hearts?

And she's off again…

Jasmine Rose:

The rat race is hectic and people don't feel that they have the time or energy. Die Mense *are usually worried that the victim has not forgiven and might seek revenge. It is more often the perpetrators who try to exact punishment against the victim, for daring to fight back and survive. Society should be worrying about whether the victim is safe and okay, and whether they are going to stay that way.*

I don't agree with her completely but Charlotte Brontë had some words to say on the matter in Jane Eyre:

'When we are struck at without a reason, we should strike back again very hard; I am sure we should – so hard as to teach the person who struck us never to do it again.'

Maybe sometimes 'An eye for an eye' DOES make more sense than 'turn the other cheek'.

And when the victim is so hurt and traumatized should someone else not step in and do the striking back? That is what happens in tribes. The Elders step in and deliberate and then send in the warriors if necessary. Especially if strong action means that the vulnerable will be protected and their community and society prevented from decaying completely?

And there is surely nothing wrong with a bit of Social Justice where the victims are heard and supported? The philosophy of 'turning the other cheek' doesn't mean make yourself deaf and heartless.

Rodin surprised me by planning a holiday trip to Cape Town over Christmas and New Year. He scraped together his allowance, got a holiday job, and borrowed from his mother to buy plane tickets for the two of us.

The holiday job was delivering Christmas presents for the famous diamond magnate, Oppenheimer, to his head executives, business partners and so on. We drove around in a white van full of *Chivas Regal* and *Moet* champagne, dropping off the hampers in the wealthy, opulent areas of Johannesburg. We fantasized about all the diamonds that these people must have touched and sold. Maybe some Blood Diamonds? We ranted about the unfairness to the African miners and people. We nattered about Colonial British Imperialism stripping the wealth and sending all the resources to the UK and Europe. We argued about how the African people are so easily corrupted when they gain control of their own resources, and how they tend not to help each other once they are in power. We agreed that it seems to be a general human trait at the moment which only the few act against.

Rodin's family were very liberal and involved in The Struggle. Rodin knew how to do the Toi-toi protest dance and had taken part in demonstrations against the Apartheid Regime. We wanted to 'Free Mandela' and thought that we should put a printed note to that effect in with the Christmas champagne for the execs. It was fun but crazy. I was a star on the stage that these people begged autographs from at Gala events, but here I was delivering Christmas pressies! I suppose being Oppenheimer's servant does have some status to it. Rodin got the gig because his family's connection to the rich and powerful Diamond Empire.

That odd-job earned us money and led up to our romantic holiday in Cape Town over the New Year. We were to stay at my ex-flatmate Vera's family home in Cape Town, which was handy because she lived by the sea and near my friend Eliza.

In the Wings

Rodin and I were in high spirits. We were recovering from all the drama. We chatted, giggled and laughed all the way to Cape Town, sending up the air hostesses and flight procedures. Despite everything I was deliriously happy. It was so weird to feel completely unhappy and traumatized, but so joyful and in love at the same time. I felt like I was being pulled in two. But thank goodness for the happiness of the relationship, otherwise suicide might have felt like the only option.

But as usual, other trouble was brewing...

I knew that part of the reason why Rodin's mother had lent the money for the trip was because she wanted Rodin to do a bit of a reconnaissance and get the lie of the land in Cape Town. He had got 'Call-Up' papers for the army and, as liberal conscientious objectors who were opposed to the Apartheid Regime, they did not want to send him to the army where he would land up fighting against the African people. He would have to fight against his own fellow citizens who were right to protest. If he went to study at the Drama School in Cape Town, he would be able to avoid the army. So that meant he would be leaving me. We discussed it and were strongly determined that our relationship could last the distance.

When we arrived in Cape Town the reception was mixed. Vera's parents were delighted to meet Rodin, but not particularly happy to see me. They clearly blamed me for my father's nonsense and I got booted out within a couple of days.

They said that an unknown female in the house was not good for their son who had 'emotional problems'. Maybe this was true. But they may have thought that I was a show-offy ballerina when I was just trying to entertain the boy with tricks at the pool. Maybe they didn't like that he knew that Rodin and I were sleeping together in their house. But they basically did to me what they felt my father had done to their daughter, i.e. forced her from her home. I had to 'pay for the sins of the father'.

So the upshot of it was that I was told to leave. Thankfully I was given sanctuary at Eliza's house and Rodin and I met as often as we could. We took long walks and made love in the dunes. The separation made our feelings stronger and we planned romantic trysts.

One night Eliza, Rodin and I planned an exciting trip to the beach. Rodin sneaked off after lights-out and joined us at Eliza's. Her parents were sleeping and we pushed her car silently out of the garage onto the drive and closed the double garage doors so as not to wake them. We now felt safe to start up the car and quietly drive off for our beach picnic. She switched on the headlights and:

Hooooooooooonk!

She panicked, hands waving. We shout-whispered, "Switch off, switch off!"

She switched off the ignition, then tried to start up again. It was fine, but as soon as she put on the headlights:

Hooooooooooooonk!

We finally did the maths and worked out that her car had been serviced that day and the mechanic must have done something odd with the wiring. The car was like a reflection of the many people in my life. Faulty wiring. We weren't about to give up on our adventure though, and drove to the beach with just the fog lights on.

In the Wings

At Blouberg Beach we put down our blankets and pillows and made ourselves a little nest in a sheltered corner with our picnic. We talked into the wee hours and at sunrise, and low tide, we walked across to the island and admired the colourful worlds within the rock pools. It was healthy for Rodin to have some good natural fun. He had been caught up in very dark, negative eighties materialism within Johannesburg. Drugs, sex, street-fighting, gangs and rock 'n' roll. I was a nature fairy who wanted to do Community Theatre work for the greater good. It was a positive experience for him to have a different perspective. He did the man-thing and told me that he thought that I was 'away with the fairies', but he enjoyed it for a bit.

Rodin got tickets for the New Year Party at the *Rondebosch Theatre*. I pulled together a glamorous outfit out of a white and gold material. It was actually a soft tube lampshade cover that had once been a sari from the Indian market. Us dancers were good at creating glamorous outfits for cheap. In a warm country you can create a stunning designer outfit from high heels and a scarf.

The food trays and champagne filled the foyer after the show. The disco was thumping and we boogied in high spirits, working up a steamy sweat. We wandered out one of the side doors onto a patio alongside the garden. We admired the massive giant fig trees with their artistic, sculptured-looking air-roots and I told Rodin about how they lined the river on the family farm.

We perched on a bench and looked up at the stars. This was a favourite pastime of ours. We started doing this on our first date. We went to a club in Johannesburg and stood on the roof trying to identify constellations. It was our habit to spot the Southern Cross and Orion's Belt wherever we were.

Rodin looked at me, took a deep breath and said:

"I love you."

At that exact moment a rat ran across in front of us.

I exclaimed:

"There's a rat!" and laughed nervously.

His first declaration of love and I didn't say I love you back! Maybe I smelled a rat – or maybe I had just been hurt too much by people who said they loved me. Tainted love.

My life had been so dark that I struggled to even say, or write, the word 'love'.

I couldn't say it back - yet – but I would. I was positive about life. I was finally free from my prison. I would finally be free to explore life. Maybe I wouldn't feel so alien anymore…

I would heal myself and learn to trust love. The only four letter word I didn't know was LOVE, but I would learn. This was the end of an Alpha and Omega cycle, but I was starting all over. Everything was new. I was like a newborn child. I was going to learn what life was all about.

You can't always choose the music that life plays for you, but once you have a little freedom, you can choose how to dance to it. I would spread my wings and dance in the skies.

I would finally be free to experience LOVE, LIGHT and LIFE.

In the Wings

This was not the end, it was just the beginning... This was the start of my Venus Rising.

I was still to travel the world, meet the hero Mandela, build *Butterfly Haven Centre* for survivors, mentor an International Youth Empowerment group and much, much more...

Denise's story continues in Book Two of the Venus Rising Series:

Behind the Scenes

World Adventures of the Alien Ballerina

Denise dances, has the honour of wearing Margot Fonteyn's tutu, and explores Eastern Spiritual Paths. She bundu-bashes through the breathtaking wilderness of South Africa before heading off to Bophuthatswana and a European Tour. There is a romantic engagement in Venice, as well as an Indian Island tour with bizarre happenings...

She shares more outrageous anecdotes and tells how she escapes a revolution and bombings. We gain more insight into the mysterious and magical world of Ballet and Dance. We join her quest for healing and her journey through therapy, self-help and personal development. She finally meets the hero Mandela.

Denise is joined in this book by Margaret McRose, Dusky Rose and others. Yup that's right people. Outrageous Jasmine is not alone. It's the invasion of a Bunch of Roses! Close Encounters of the prickly kind...

Denise Stephani

Free at Last!
Flying in the skies...

In the Wings

Thank you for hearing my story.

This is me, age 5, just after the 'monster' turned up.

Base make-up and pink tights were covering my bruised legs and rear. I was already well trained to put on a mask and smile through the pain.

Shut up, put up and stiff upper lip...

Jasmine Rose:

A.D. – After Disaster!

(Photo by a well-known international photographer. The shoot was for a full page newspaper advert for carpets.)

Epilogue

Okay – so you get that my life was yuk, bleergh, aaargh, with a few dance recitals in between. So how did I cope and still succeed in life and career and not turn out to be a total wreck?

This is what the book is about. I'm not trying to impart my misery upon the world. I am trying to share the coping strategies, the signs of abuse to look out for, and the truths of all those suffering this silent curse which is destroying the world. Everything is connected, and the destruction of environment and economy is all connected to this abusive, bullying, taking attitude which prevails.

I am trying to share a tale of inspiration. Of maintaining hope and positivity, despite hardship, and becoming a fully-rounded, contributing citizen, working for the greater good at a time when the planet needs it desperately. I am not attention seeking or looking for fame. I want to do good. Even if I made some money out of this, it would never pay back the decades of suffering and the fourteen years it took to write it. It would never make up for going back into Post Traumatic Stress during the writing process with nightmares and abdominal pain. It would never give back the social and family time sacrificed. A large portion of royalties will be going into a fund to continue the good work and help suffering children and survivors to cope and heal. The research and writing of this book which has taken a toll on me is a sacrifice for the Evolution of the Community of Humankind.

My survival strategies were to read up and inform myself of what was happening. As soon as I could recognize words, I started reading, to understand what was

In the Wings

happening to me and what was going on in this strange world.

I read about a horrific abuse case when I was just eight years old. It was an account of a boy who was locked in a small caravan cupboard, tortured with electrical shocks and eventually died as a result. I realized that I was not alone. The *Reader's Digest* also gave some abuse statistics and I realized that there were millions of us out there in the world going through similar things. More than a third of the people you meet have been badly abused, and we've all been abused in some way or another. So I decided that one day I would do something about it. My journey to help uplift the suffering millions started then.

Through my journey over the decades I have realized that there is a great pressure from the advantaged to keep the disadvantaged suffering. Even the people working in Aid Organisations often seem to be more invested in keeping people down in their victim box to be lorded over, rather than uplifting them.

My message to the world is that it doesn't have to be like this. There is way too much unnecessary suffering in this world even if you go with the theory that it is a 'Soul University' and that God works in mysterious ways. We could be co-creating something so much better, and in many ways it is just a matter of a mind shift and reaching out to each other. We need to make the world a place where women and children and the good guys, the global majority, can live and thrive in the way that they would like to live. Currently, even abuse survivors themselves tend to perpetuate abuse and misery, or are disinclined to help each other or be involved in inspiring change: "We suffered and survived in silence, so let others suffer and survive too!"

It is enough people. Let's draw a line and do something different!

So how did I survive all this without going mad? Bottom line?

It's a miracle. But a self-created miracle.

It boils down to a few things:

The Arts, Creativity and Nature.

I made sure that I used all forms of the arts for self-expression even though I couldn't talk about what was happening to me. I danced, read, wrote, watched great film, drew and examined the world.

I did not wallow in my own case of human rights violation and injustice and use it as an excuse to opt out of life. I looked around and saw how much of it was in the world around me – and I took active steps to do something about it. I used all my talents and worked to change the world around me and make a difference. And when people obstructed and wouldn't help – I said, "Fuck 'em", and carried on anyway! SOMEBODY had to care. So let it be me.

When people around me were cruel, nasty, indifferent, mean-spirited and sabotaging, I side-stepped with a big beaming smile and continued on my mission of 'Niceness'! I knew that it takes more strength to remain good and kind in adversity than it does to become all bitter and twisted, shut-down, selfish and pathetic.

I knew that there was a cycle to break and I broke it! I'm not saying I'm perfect, as the work on the damage is ongoing, but I have done the best I can.

I watched my parents and analysed and assessed them. I looked at their behaviour and I decided for myself which behaviour was wrong and mad. Then I made a conscious effort to do the opposite.

I want to start an 'Order of the Rose' like Christine de Pizan did in the 1400s calling for higher aspirations, loyalty, respect and honouring of the humans who bring us into the world. I want to create Awards for people who have survived horrible life trauma to honour them - a chance for the Downtrodden to feel heard.

Ha ha! lol. Maybe the Order of Jasmine Rose? ☺

It happens to boys too.

Here is the true story offered by a very good friend of mine:

It was great time in the life of a young boy who loved his ballet. He joined a major ballet school in his country. When he arrived, the excitement of dancing eight hours a day, all the different styles and people he met, was overwhelming.

I was only seventeen. I'd been enjoying all that new environment, going out like all young teenage boys, going to parties. Like any teenage boy I was thinking about girls and there was no shortage of beautiful young ladies. However, I was very shy and one thing my dad had taught me was to be very respectful of women and that is something I've kept in mind all my life. I went out with one or two girls (just as friends) from the school, went to parties and I was very careful not to drink too much.

Denise Stephani

What I remember of my second year at the school is that I was doing okay with the school workload; however, in the second year, not long after attending a party, I become very distracted and started struggling with the course work. I was continually calling home saying, "I want to come home." I kept saying to mum and dad I missed home and needed to come home. They didn't - and still don't know - the whole truth of my reason for coming home.

The story: I went to a party. I was running to catch a train with a group of dancers like we did every Saturday afternoon; we were going to lunch before being extras in a performance with the Dance Company. This went like all other performances as an extra. That night there was a party we were all going to. It was not far from where I lived.

However, all I remember is waking up in a bed while a man was sucking me off and this freaked me out. I pushed the man off me, still feeling groggy. I freaked out, and remembered asking: "What the fuck have you done to me?" But he said, "Only what you asked for."

I got very angry, shouting, "I would never have agreed to this! I only had two drinks, so what did you give me?"

His denial just kept going on and on so I demanded he tell me where I was and give me enough money to get me home. I remember it was about $50.00 which back in the 70s was a lot of money. I went home in the taxi which took nearly one hour so this meant I had been taken very far from the party and home.

I noticed that my bum was very sore. I could only guess what had just happened to me. That man must have doped me somehow, because otherwise I would have fought back.

On the following day I saw the person who attacked me. He was the wardrobe master of the Ballet Company. This was very uncomfortable for me and I struggled with the difficult emotions caused by what had happened. I was only young, and I knew that no one would believe what had happened to me.

As the days and weeks went on I lost all interest in dancing. I said to my parents that I was homesick and needed to come home. I didn't finish the last year of the course and went home, keeping all of this to myself. Even up until today there are only a couple of people that know what happened - and only one that now knows the whole story.

As I think back about this time you could say I lost my innocence to a monster. However, in my mind I lost my innocence with a beautiful ballet dancer (I was about 20 years old, about two years after my rape) which I joined not long after I left the school.

There is one thing I must say: Over the past 30 years I have nothing against gay persons. However, like with all other groups there will be these monsters, child molesters, rapists etc.

The question I often ask myself is: is this still affecting me today?

Over the past 30 years or so, like many people, I've had my ups and downs; I would say more downs than ups; I only had a couple of relationships in the first ten years after the attack and none since then.

This is the story of many boys and young men. He didn't give up and allow himself to be 'made gay'. He didn't buy into the belief that a woman wouldn't want him after that. He wasn't caught up in the decadence and the easily available sex.

He has suffered depression and physical illness as a result of his experience for decades. It is usual for survivors to suffer digestive and bowel problems, but he has maintained hope and continues to work on his healing. He now bravely tells his story.

He deserves a medal for Bravery and Valour. For being a Man of Honour in a dishonourable world.

Coming soon...

The World According to Jasmine Rose

Jasmine's Poetry about Love and Romance

Inspired by love troubles and online relationship advice...

<u>*A Women's Celebration of the End of a Misguided Love*</u>

It would be so great NOT to ever see you again.

NEVER AGAIN to feel that confusion and pain...

Not to feel your presence,

Not to hear your voice,

Not to have ANYTHING to do with your games and nonsense.

Phew! The sigh of relief,

Over and over again.

I want to be like a man.

I want to fight to be 'empty' and 'free'.

I want to deny connection like a man,

Avoid love at all costs,

THAT DREADED SCARY THING.

I will ignore all desire for a life partner,

Whom I can be a team with.

I will wend my lonely way –

Putting myself on the pedestal of my own ego.

I will revel in my arrogant busy-ness,

Far too important for the mere trappings of love,

Far too impressive and career-driven to have fun!
To have a life...
This is me,
I am now a man.

Inspired by love disappointment and the disappearance of the Chinese Mail Order Bride next door:

<u>*Sad Song Of The Mail Order Bride Who Got Sent Back*</u>

He wished for me...
He visualized...
He longed for his perfect partner.
But when I arrived he didn't recognize me.
"Send it back!" he said.
"I want a Japanese Love Doll instead."
That is the perfect partner.
Silent and available.
Allows me to be solo ruler.
I want no Queen to mar the perfection of my Kingship.
Let me pleasure my dick in plastic,
And send that annoyance back!

The World According to Jasmine Rose will be available as e-book and paperback soon

Coming soon...

Abuse Guide

After decades of research and experience, Denise says it like it is, and gives help and advice to survivors.

Below is a poem expressing the feelings of children and survivors:

From My Inner Child

Questions and thoughts from my childhood:

*C*an my mommy love me if she lets him do this to me?

*H*ow have I made them angry and caused this punishment for myself?

I must have done something wrong.

*L*ook at what he's doing to me. Listen to my cries for help.

*D*id I do something terrible to God so that he has turned his back on me?

*A*m I to blame for what is happening?

*B*ruises all over - but not as bruised as my heart...

*U*nclean. Unloved. Unlovable.

*S*ex toy. I wish I was a boy so I wouldn't be his sex toy.

*E*very day is pain.

This poem and other writing were contributed to the book *Survivor Moms* and newsletter produced by Mickey Sperlich, a compassionate midwife. Mickey was inspired to do this from all her years of seeing the side effects of abuse which hit new mothers the worst when they are pregnant, birthing and raising their children.
www.survivormoms.com

The abuse guide will contain current and past statistics:

Example:

Facts about domestic violence and abuse

Conservative figures posted by Sherna Alexander Benjamin (cause founder) from the 'I am saying no to Domestic Abuse' Cause http://www.facebook.com/profile.php?id=1526365778#!/sayingnotoabuse

One in every four women will experience domestic violence in her lifetime. (One in three children are abused.) An estimated 1.3 million women are victims of physical assault by an intimate partner each year. 85% of domestic violence victims are women.

Historically, females have been most often victimized by someone they knew.

Females who are 20-24 years of age are at the greatest risk of non-fatal intimate partner violence. Most cases of domestic violence are never reported to the police.

CHILDREN WHO WITNESS

Witnessing violence between one's parents or caretakers is the strongest risk factor of transmitting violent behaviour from one generation to the next. Boys who witness domestic violence are twice as likely to abuse their own partners and children when they become adults. 30% to 60% of perpetrators of intimate partner violence also abuse children in the household.

HOMICIDE AND INJURY

Almost one-third of female homicide victims that are reported in police records are killed by an intimate partner. In 70-80% of intimate partner homicides, no matter which partner was killed, the man physically abused the woman before the murder. Less than one-fifth of victims reporting an injury from intimate partner violence sought medical treatment following the injury. Intimate partner violence results in more than 18.5 million mental health care visits each year.

SEXUAL ASSAULT AND STALKING

One in 6 women and 1 in 33 men have experienced an attempted or completed rape.

Nearly 7.8 million women have been raped by an intimate partner at some point in their lives. Sexual assault or forced sex occurs in approximately 40-45% of battering relationships. 1 in 12 women and 1 in 45 men have been stalked in their lifetime.

81% of women stalked by a current or former intimate partner are also physically assaulted by that partner; 31% are also sexually assaulted by that partner.

ECONOMIC IMPACT

The cost of intimate partner violence exceeds $5.8 billion each year, $4.1 billion of which is for direct medical and mental health services. Victims of intimate partner violence lost almost 8 million days of paid work because of the violence perpetrated against them by current or former husbands, boyfriends and dates. This loss is the equivalent of more than 32,000 full-time jobs and almost 5.6 million days of household productivity as a result of violence.

There are 16,800 homicides and 2.2 million (medically treated) injuries due to intimate partner violence annually, which costs $37 billion.

Denise Stephani

REPORTING RATES

Domestic violence is one of the most chronically under-reported crimes. Only approximately one-quarter of all physical assaults, one-fifth of all rapes, and one-half of all stalkings perpetrated against females by intimate partners are reported to the police.

These are American and First World Conservative Figures. In South Africa and other countries the figures are MUCH worse.

South Africa has the highest Sexual Violence statistics in the World. Some statistics examples are: One rape every 23 seconds and 11 women a day killed by their own husband or partner: More than 4,000 per year, representing a general culture of Gendercide.

Abuse Guide is well researched with statistics and quotes from a variety of experts. It is highly recommended for parents, teachers, therapists, volunteers, medical practitioners, social and community workers and will be available as e-book and paperback soon.

In the Wings

Butterfly Haven Children's Fund

Butterfly Haven Castle Center, Cape Town, South Africa

This centre hosted fundraising projects, and was the base for 'Kids Can'– The South African branch of Free the Children initiated and mentored by Denise Stephani for 7 years. www.freethechildren.com This International network was started by Craig and Marc Kielberger in Canada, originally to help free child slaves. It has moved on to be a powerful international youth empowerment and citizenship network, and has been nominated for the Nobel Peace Prize. It has been part of Oprah's Angel Network and mentored by Bishop Desmond Tutu, Richard Gere, Kuki Gallman and many more.

Butterfly Haven Centre was closed in 2007 due to the extreme violent crime levels and lack of support.

Butterfly Haven Enchanted Castle Playpark and projects were enjoyed by many children. Sadly it was a dream that died because of the "Beetles" and "Nasties".

However, the vision continues in the UK with the new Butterfly Haven Children's Fund and proceeds from this book which raises awareness and educates on abuse, and it's devastating effects on society – as well as helping survivors of abuse.

Acknowledgement & Thanks

Thank you to Edinburgh University Office of Life Long Learning, AMORC

and Fluid Eye Productions for Writing, Psychology and Film Training.

A big thank you to the following people, who had the courage to give me a little verbal support and help during the creating of this community book, film and dance project. They didn't close a door in my face or try to exploit. (I'm sorry if I sound bitter, but it has been a long, tough journey for this 'elephant in the room'.)

A few words of encouragement or advice are free to give,

but precious pearls to the receiver, which far too many hold back...

Steinvor Palsson, Craig Burgess, Vincent Hantam, Isobel Ross, Emma Jones, Katy McKoewn, Dr Femi Foloronso, Edwina Sheridan, Bob Martin, Janelle French, Agnes Ness, Judy Adams, Sitar Rose, Dr Colin Cooper, Leon Moodley, Colleen Pope, Margit Forssman, Dr Pauline Nolan, Hayley Roberts, Emily Streete, Joanne Pirrie and Aaron Jeffrey, Sue Hampson and all my dance clients.

Also fellow writers:
Warren Glover, Monique Rockcliffe, Megan Voysey, Hyan Thiboutot, Ishbel McCormack,
Amy Williamson, Iman Murrar, Mark Prebble and Marion Shortt
My Boys for giving mom writing time and understanding:
Xavier Angel and Aikiyo Gabriel, and also Bruce Luke

Photography: Bob Martin, Jean-Claude Mousset, Gavin Furlonger and Tali Yankelavich

Healing Scottish Nature and Tourism places where I wrote: Portobello, Joppa, Aberdour, Burntisland, Linlithgow, Loch Lomond, Stirling, Findhorn, North Berwick, South Queensferry, Water of Leith, Dunblane

A few of the Precious Pearls which kept me going:

"Wow – this is so powerful, the passion and inspiration shines through."

"A worthy contribution"

"Think of how many people you will be able to help"

"Very brave, good and true"

In the Wings

Coming soon...

Book 2

Behind the Scenes

World Adventures of the Alien Ballerina

Book 3

Butterfly Haven Castle

Alien Ballerina Creates a New World

Children's Books:

Letters to Mandela

This book contains beautiful Pictures and Writing from children all over South Africa and in Scotland. They express their sadness about violence and abuse and describe the World that they would like to inherit. A brief overview of the Apartheid Regime, Transformation, and the New South Africa. It is designed as a children's book and educational resource.

The Tale of Butterfly Haven Castle

The Enchanting Tale of Butterfly Haven Castle. When children visited they were given an Olde Map and taken on a tour of the magical kingdom. They were told a marvellous tale of all the spritely forest folk and characters living in this mystic world. The book illustrations combine photos and art.

These books are suitable for children of a range of ages from all over the world.

This list of books is highly recommended for parents, teachers, therapists, volunteers, medical practitioners, social and community workers and will be available as e-book and paperback soon.

Research and Recommended Reading:

(There will be a more extensive reading and website list in Denise's upcoming book: *Guide to Abuse and Life Trauma* and online.)

Therapy and Abuse

Survivor Moms – Women's Stories of Birthing, Mothering and Healing after Sexual Abuse

By Mickey Sperlich, MA, CPM and Julia S. Seng, PHD, CNM

Motherbaby Press ISBN 978 -1-89-044641-3

(Contains writing and contributions from Denise Stephani after the birth of her first child in 2000)
www.survivormoms.com

The Courage to Heal – A Guide for Women Survivors of Child Sexual Abuse

By Ellen Bass & Laura Davis

Vermillion ISBN 0 7493 0938 5

Puzzling People: The Labyrinth of the Psychopath

By Thomas Sheridan

Velluminous Press ISBN: 978-1-905605-28-6

Why men don't listen and women can't read maps

By Allan & Barbara Pease

Orion books Limited ISBN 0 75284 619 1

Women who run with the Wolves
By Clarissa Pinkola Estes
Random House ISBN 0 7126 7134 X
Novel re abuse in Private Schools:
Top of the World
By James W. Mitchell
JSM Press ISBN-10: 0955425808

Spiritual

How to Know God
By Deepak Chopra
Random House ISBN 07126 7035 I

The Heart Sutra
By Osho
Element ISBN 1-85230-477-4

History & Social Reform

The Order of the Rose – the life and ideas of Christine de Pizan
By Enid McLeod
Chatto & Windus ISBN: 0 7011 1927 6

AWA' AN' BILE YER HEID - Scottish Curses & Insults
Barbara Robertson & David Ross
Interlink Publishing Group
ISBN-10: 1841582441

Websites:

www.denisestephani.com

Denise Stephani on Youtube:

http://www.youtube.com/user/denisestephani?feature=mhee

Culture of Abuse Magazine:

www.cultureofabuse.com/?page_id=2

www.survivormoms.com

www.freethechildren.com

For information about Valentina, Rwandan Refugee, Google search:

Valentina of the Rwandan Genocide

http://www.un.org/en/preventgenocide/rwanda/testimonies/pdf/7%20-%20Valentina%202009.pdf

Denise Stephani